A Provocative Discussion for and About Gay Men
Seeking Empowerment and Internal Satisfaction

YOU'VE BEEN BLOCKED

The Search for Gay Male Perfection

JOSEPH CONTORER, MA

The Collateral Press
LOS ANGELES

Published by
The Collateral Press
LOS ANGELES, CA
www.theblockedbook.com

Copyright © 2025 Joseph Contorer

All rights reserved.

No part of this publication may be reproduced, stored in a retrieval system, or transmitted in any form or by any means, electronic, mechanical, photocopying, recording, or otherwise, without prior written permission from the publisher.

The information presented is the author's opinion and does not constitute any health or medical advice. The content of this book is for informational purposes only and is not intended to diagnose, treat, cure, or prevent any condition or disease.

ISBNs: 979-8-9902934-5-8   (Paperback)
       979-8-9902934-6-5   (Hardcover)
       979-8-9902934-7-2   (Ebook)
       979-8-9902934-8-9   (Audiobook)

Library of Congress Control Number 2024905073

Cover design by Tracie Crowser
Interior layout by Gary A. Rosenberg

The author may be reached at: Joseph@theblockedbook.com

M-Ranking® is a registered trademark of Joseph Contorer

Contents

Introduction..1

PART I   Being Blocked During Gay Childhood

1. DIMENSION #1: Home, Parents, and Family Form the Basis of Being Blocked..9

2. DIMENSION #2: School, Community, and Society Continue and Compound the Blocking Process........................15

3. Being Blocked in Adolescence Causes Various Reactions.......19

4. Invalidation and Shame Magnification Are the Cause and Consequence of Being Blocked........................25

PART II   Blocking in the Adult Gay Male Community

5. DIMENSION #3: The Adult Gay Male Community (GMC)..........39

6. The M-Ranking® Search for Male Perfection Creates Cutthroat Judging in the GMC...............................47

7. M-RANKING #1: Masculinity Is the Composite and Core of the M-Ranking System 55

8. M-RANKING #2: Manhood—Penis Size, Sexual Appeal, and Performance 63

9. M-RANKING #3: Model Looks and Muscles, Youthfulness, and the Power of Visual Perfection.........................69

10. M-RANKING #4: Money and Material Wealth Can Supplement Other M-Ranking Values 79

11. M-RANKING #5: Mainstream Compatibility in Both Straight and Gay Environments 83

PART III Ramifications of Straight Male Privilege on Gay Men

12. Straight Male Privilege: A Different Life of Unforeseen Advantages for Heterosexual Men 89

13. I'm Almost Positive: The Striking Impact of HIV/AIDS 103

PART IV Characterological Consequences and the Narcissistic Spectrum in the Gay Male Community

14. Narcissism in the GMC 115

15. Identity Confusion, Disorders, and Narcissism in Gay Men 133

16. Defense Mechanisms and Delusions 137

17. Alcoholic Thinking, Alcoholic Behavior, the Pleasure Principle, and Similar Compulsions 145

PART V Choice Information

18. Choices and Boundaries 155

19. The Closet Conundrum: Stay in or Come Out? 159

PART VI Unlocking and Unblocking Solutions and Resolutions

20. The Unblocking Factor (U-Factor): Maximizing Internal Satisfaction 169

21. Insightful and Informed Versus Shallow, Detached, and Unaware 175

22. Integrity and Humility: Independence and Individuality 181

23. Intimacy 187

Conclusion 197

Endnotes 201

Index 207

About the Author 215

*For my parents, Paul and Beverly who blessed me
with many gifts for resilience and success,*

*and Joseph Contorer, 1867–1941,
who paved the way by coming to America,*

*and beloved friends, Chip, Brian, Jennifer,
Robert, Kent, Diane, Christine, Richard,
and several others who left too soon*

Introduction

The term *gay* is a descriptor for homosexuals and is frequently used to reference homosexual men or women who self-identify as having and being of homosexual (same-sex) orientation. The use of the term *homosexual* has brought controversy, as it was formerly classified as a mental illness; it is a concise description that refers to those generally included in what is currently referred to as the lesbian, gay, bisexual, transgender, and questioning (LGBTQ+) community. The term is referenced here for objective factual clarity and comparison. Homosexual orientation for a male includes same-sex attraction romantically, physically, and sexually to other males. One estimate from a 2024 Gallop Poll suggests that gay men represent a vast minority of Americans, approximately 2.1%.[1]

Initially, young gay boys are almost always systematically inhibited—or what I refer to as being blocked—because most parents assume and commonly prefer that their children are heterosexual. When gay boys are blocked, they are less able to naturally express, develop, or interact in an authentic, unaffected manner. Most young gay boys do not have the cognitive capacity to identify what "gay" is or means or that they are gay; this identity becomes more evident as they progress through the various stages of childhood development, particularly in adolescence. Parental expectations are based on a presumption that all boys are a specific, standardized, heterosexual version of what "normal" is. Heterosexuality is a standard norm that is also modeled and reflected in educational, community, and religious affiliations.

The Gay Male Community (GMC) Within the LGBTQ+ Community

You've Been Blocked analyzes commonly observed dynamics and related interactions among gay men. It is also a navigation tool for them and those who wish to understand them better. The goal is to empower gay men with improved insight and internal acceptance. Conclusions or solutions, if applicable, will be up to individual readers.

The group of gay men within the LGBTQ+ community is collectively referred to here as the gay male community (GMC). The GMC refers to adult homosexual men over the age of 18 (unless adolescents/minors are mentioned or referred to specifically). The LGBTQ+ community is inclusive of gay men and gay women, yet the GMC includes specific variables and unique issues about neighborhoods, communities/social scenes, norms, and dynamics mainly relative to gay men interacting with one another as opposed to gay women, transgender people, bisexuals, or those who might identify as "questioning" or nonbinary and other designations.

The discussion is based on my own experiences and conclusions. The GMC is a broad term here that technically comprises all men who are gay, regardless of their self-disclosure and how open any individual gay man chooses to be or how officially connected to a gay male community they are.

Ironically, blocking continues in a different capacity in the GMC. As a health educator and clinician, I have professionally and personally observed and experienced patterns of behaviors and traits that are unique to gay men. Much of the dynamic in the GMC originates from a different childhood development than that of the majority of their straight peers. *You've Been Blocked* is a discussion that explores the experiences of gay men and the relevant topics affecting them. Welcome to the conversation.

You've Been Blocked Is Written with Several Intentions

- **The book is an explanatory, proactive resource guide** for gay men and is intended to support gay men, some of whom are in therapy or recovery.

- **It is beneficial reading material for anyone,** across many segments of society, culture, gender, religion, and ethnicity, who is willing to become informed about some of the complexities that impact gay men.

- **Readers can increase awareness** and understanding of the impact of scrutiny on gay men.

- **There is still substantial ignorance about gay boys/men.** Society, including portions of families of gay men, has generally been misinformed and sometimes hateful and intolerant.

- **Treatment of gay men has improved, but they are still** often treated differently from straight men. Society has become more exposed to gay men; however, gay men still have a higher likelihood than straight men of facing negative stigmas and prejudices.

- **Blocking creates profound differences for gay men** as compared to straight men. Gay boys and later, gay men, have a complex, repressive experience directly related to being blocked.

- **Gay boys engage in self-repression;** they often repress their true gay selves until they "know better," but by then, they are part of a well-greased machine of being blocked and blocking themselves. Because of this process, many are what I refer to as "damaged by default."

- **Most gay boys are initially presumed to be straight** for various time periods. Most are presumed to be heterosexual from the time they are born and are groomed as such.

- **Gay boys learn to comfort others as a mechanism** of self-protection. They feel the need to please and accommodate others. This starts with self-repression, but backfires in multiple ways in later years, damaging their self-worth.
- **Unblocking may help achieve clarity and empowerment.** Recovery from childhood trauma is a complex process that requires improving a sense of self-worth and resolving historical blockage.

You've Been Blocked Is Written for Gay Men and on Behalf of Gay Men

You've Been Blocked is also geared toward those in therapy or recovery programs, as well as clinicians and therapists. The material is beneficial for family, friends, and other supporters.

Society Presumes All Boys Are Straight and Disparages Many Who Are Gay

Male homosexuals, in particular, have been subjected to hostile, unfair, and abusive treatment. Society has maintained preconceived expectations for how *all* males are presumed to be straight, which equates to what is considered "normal" by many.

Even the idea of or reference to gay men has been commonly depicted negatively. Generally speaking, there is a predisposed, systemic, covert (microaggressive), and overt (macroaggressive) pressure that presumes all boys (even if they are gay or found out to be gay or come out as gay later) are and should be heterosexual boys. Gay men need to come to terms with the reality that some degree of anti-gay bias may always be present. The sometimes-critical response to differences in sexual identity is a less flattering part of human nature.

Progress Has Been Made in Society Toward Being More "Gay Affirmative," but There Is Still Much Room for Improvement

Portions of society have become more aware, tolerant, and "gay affirmative." However, for many gay men, the damage has been done; current advancement won't simply resolve the impact of a long-standing history. I believe this is particularly relevant to gay men born before 1980 or so. In the 2020s, these men are likely between 40 and 80+ years old. It is also my opinion that many older gay men (those born before 1970 or so) have suffered even more damage because of critical societal values pertaining to homosexual men.

Critical Thinking Choice Checkpoints

Throughout the book, you will see the icon below. These are visual signposts to alert readers to key concepts.

> **CRITICAL THINKING CHOICE CHECKPOINT #1**
>
> An objective of *You've Been Blocked* is to show that resolving the impact and history of gay boys and gay men who have been blocked does not ultimately have a comprehensive, unilateral solution. Individuals will have to do that work and come to their own conclusions.

Topics and Questions Covered by *You've Been Blocked*

- **What is "blocking,"** and how and why do many gay boys eventually partake in the blocking process themselves?

- **What is it like growing up as a gay boy?** How does this experience differ from straight boys?

- **How does the cutting power of shame and invalidation** versus empowerment, self-acceptance, and affirmativeness often lead to underachieving and emotional damage?

- **Why do many gay men feel like they are never good enough?** Why do gay men often feel like "have-nots" instead of "haves"?

- **How does the extensive focus on masculinity create a search for male perfection** in the gay male community and a rating system that I call "the M-Ranking®?"

- **Why are some gay men more prone to narcissism** and similar personality traits or disorders?

- **Why do gay men often have self-destructive substance abuse problems?**

- **How is unblocking accomplished?** How might gay men begin to "unblock" themselves, and how can society support this effort?

- **Why and how do straight or gay people** make choices, such as gay men choosing whether to come out and be openly gay or straight people choosing to become informed and more tolerant about what and who gay men are?

PART I

Being Blocked During Gay Childhood

CHAPTER 1

DIMENSION #1: Home, Parents, and Family Form the Basis of Being Blocked

Dimension #1 begins for gay boys at home when children primarily interface with their parents and family. This is where blocking initiates. During this crucial phase, many parents and families will not create an adequate support system for their son who, they will later discover, is gay. These boys are mostly unable to be their authentic selves.

In Dimension #1, parents and family frequently presume or prefer that their boys will be heterosexual or "straight." Presuming or hoping that a gay boy is straight is oppressive and non-affirming.

The fact is that gay boys are *not straight*; they will not legitimately identify as heterosexual, regardless of the presumptions or false hopes of parents and family. Most of them are indoctrinated in a benign manner to be heterosexual by reinforcing stereotypical social and emotional behavioral norms that would be observed in straight boys.

Impact of Assuming All Children Are Heterosexual or Encouraging Them to Be

It is my conclusion that, despite improved awareness and tolerance of gayness, it is still common for parents to expect their children to be straight; this is referred to as a *heteronormative* process.[2] Primarily normalizing heterosexuality by default is a pattern that may not significantly change; it starts with the reality that the majority of people are, in fact, born heterosexual. Most parents are not supportive enough when they learn their child is not straight, and many block gay traits or indicators.

Parents are likely to redirect signs of what they perceive to be inappropriate gay-like or girlish behaviors, interests, and actions that some gay boys display. They may believe they are doing the right thing in dissuading any signs or implications of potential gayness in their sons.

The Blocking Process Affects Identity Development

The identity development formulated in Dimension #1 incorporates multiple factors. Sexual identity, also known as sexual orientation, is a chief component of overall self-identity. This includes personality traits, temperament, characterological preferences, visual appearance, and various interests.

I am not suggesting we should "sexualize" young children. Younger gay boys are generally not yet entirely aware of their sexual (gay) identity. Blocking a gay boy's identity development is particularly insidious because they have limited cognitive awareness to fully comprehend a gay identity, which is already juxtaposed against whatever juvenile insight they do have, plus the impact of any non-gay-affirming, deterring messages they are exposed to.

Being blocked is a traumatizing reality that virtually all gay boys will face, even in the 2020s and beyond, in supposedly more liberal, tolerant times. Gay boys are *not* straight boys, whether that is desired, fully identified, comprehended, or confirmed yet.

It is understandable, though not helpful, that some parents normalize heterosexuality as a protective function on behalf of their children, since they may fear that their gay children have a predictably harder life ahead.

Parents report that they are tolerant of learning their child may be gay.[3] In my opinion, many parents may still prefer that their family is in line with what they define as predicably normal and straight.

The alleged improved tolerance doesn't equate to an unmitigated, constructive support of gay boys, and it doesn't stop the blocking process. Many parents of gay boys reject the notion that their son is not the "normal" version that they presumed he would be. This may include disapproving of less conventionally masculine activities and interests, like playing with girls or with dolls or "dress-up" (not all gay boys necessarily have those exact interests).

Straight-Normal and Gay-Normal Are Both Normal and Abnormal

Normal is an adjective and a noun and is defined as adhering to some presumed, predictable, standardized state of being or situation. Society has maintained long-held presumptions of "normal behavior" and "normal" images of boys and men. I use the term *straight-normal* to refer to what is normative for straight boys. The dilemma is that straight-normal is still the standardized, expected normative behavior for all boys. Despite the pressure to be straight-normal, being heterosexual or "straight" is not normal for gay boys, and it shouldn't be because they are not straight! *Gay-normal* is what is normative for gay boys. However, in marked contrast, gay-normal is not generally a comfortable, available option for most gay boys nor a typical interpretation of what normal is for any boys; furthermore, gay-normal is not welcomed by the majority of boys and other peers who are straight.

Gay children deserve to have a content life, even if the vast majority of all children are not gay. When gay boys are expected to conform to the presumption of straight-normal anyway, a transcending boundary violation occurs. Generalized social norms for all men have been based on straight, heterosexual male archetypes. Straight normal is normal if you are a straight man. Many people, including some misguided gay men, adhere to the idea that straight-normal defines the meaning of being male, normal, and acceptable.

When parents reinforce the idea that normal is presumptuously based on straight-normal, a situation of "otherness" is created for gay boys. In an effort to self-protect, this dynamic eventually includes self-blocking by the gay boys themselves. Many gay boys have been manipulated to think that all boys should act only a certain (straight) way. Consequently, gay boys begin a sickening codependent process of accommodating the needs, expectations, and comfort levels of others, starting with their parents. Many gay boys attempt to conform to a generalized ideal of what they think *others* have decided is normal.

Facts and Fundamentals of Blocking Create Atypical Challenges for Gay Boys

A constructive, gay-affirming environment ultimately requires meticulous cultivation and attention by parents. Environments primarily accommodate heterosexual children since they are the sizable majority. "Best estimates suggest that between 7–9% of youth identify as lesbian, gay, bisexual, transgender, or queer."[4]

Inadequate, incompetent parenting is bound to occur. Sometimes, parents of gay boys tend to be naïve or assume they are doing the right thing by only normalizing heterosexuality and discouraging gayness.

Religious influences/fundamentalism of parents and the family's limited awareness or deficient judgment harm a developing gay boy's self-esteem. Religion and spirituality are intended to be a source of support, faith, and optimism. However, they can also be a major influence of anti-gay propaganda and reactive fear and contempt.

General dysfunction is another layer that may impact any family. This might include mental illness, abuse, addictions, poverty, chaotic outer/political unrest, major conflicts, and unstable macro social climates (like wars, financial crises, increasing "woke" political and social divisionism, and 2020's COVID disturbance).

Abuse, neglect, and boundary violations are potentially more relevant in some families. Gay boys experience higher rates of childhood abuse.[5] It is my view that gay boys are more apt to be abused because perpetrators see them as vulnerable targets. Predators may include anyone but are often within the family and sometimes found in religious organizations or other institutions with authority figures who might be struggling with sexual identity.

Self-blocking occurs when gay boys feel pressured to block themselves from the coercion to act and be "normal" (straight-normal).

Arrested development of gay boys creates long-term damage; blocking a comprehensive identity development at critical junctures interferes with proper, naturally compounding progress and innate emotional maturity.

Acting-out behaviors are revealed after gay boys are traumatized. Some become oppositional and defiant toward parents, teachers, and other authority figures. Others will underachieve or overachieve to avoid or compensate for their confusing, frightening secret. Gay boys commonly self-destruct and restrict their success and exposure by what I refer to as "invisibilizing" themselves. They fear recognition of their gayness will disappoint and offend others, especially their own parents and family.

Learning self-hatred. Feigning being straight is a self-destructive, tentative solution with long-term consequences. Gay boys are essentially taught to dislike themselves for being themselves. Then, many spend their lives trying to unlearn this distorted, self-loathing behavior. With time, some gay men may also become snarky, hateful, and judgmental about many things, including other gay men and other people.

CHAPTER 2

DIMENSION #2: School, Community, and Society Continue and Compound the Blocking Process

Until 1973, the American Psychiatric Association (APA—not to be confused with the American Psychological Association, also sometimes abbreviated as APA) considered homosexuality a psychological disorder, and "not until 1987 was the term completely removed from the (*Diagnostic and Statistical Manual*) *DSM*."[6] Being gay is *not* bad, sick, wrong, or pathological and should not be regarded as abnormal. However, being gay is also not traditionally normal.

Gay boys are attracted to other boys differently from the way straight boys interact with other straight boys. Gay boys' attraction to other boys is challenging because the majority of the other boys are *not* gay, including those the gay boys may have some attraction toward.

Gay boys have some similarities to all children, but many also have different feelings and interests than their straight male counterparts. Some gay boys are fortunate to have more tolerant parents and external/school or similarly supportive environments. Nonetheless, most are still blocked from having a safe option to freely reveal and eventually better understand and embrace what being gay means to them.

As adults, straight men and straight people are somewhat more tolerant toward gay men.[7] Childhood is a time of less forgiveness for gay boys because schoolchildren are predictably not self-restrained in their negative, critical reactions to gay peers. The treatment of gay boys was even worse in the past, when millions of adult gay men grew up being routinely tormented.

School Experiences Supersize the Blocking Process

Prior to entering school, gay boys have less interface with sources outside their immediate family. **Dimension #2** becomes an additional influence through school settings, religious affiliations, involvement in sports, and extracurricular social and community activities. Influences from Dimension #2 may continue as adult variations in the workplace or adult social spaces.

School Is Frequently a Traumatic, Unpleasant Experience for Gay Boys

Many gay boys are invalidated at school in numerous ways by peers, teachers, and the entire system. School conditions often cause penetrating emotional pain and anxiety for gay boys, who are frequently reminded through the hateful actions of others how negatively their perceived femininity and other "indicators" of gayness are viewed.

The reality is that something *is* considerably different about gay boys; their differences certainly do not mean they are immoral or wrong, nor that they should be different from who they are or "taught a lesson." Perhaps parents, teachers, or peers have been more encouraged to be less *openly* hateful about gayness in recent years; however, many are still not fully in support of promoting an affirmative perception of gay boys. Even with improved and greater tolerance, many gay boys still feel emotionally unsafe and subjected to threats

> *The reality is that something* is *considerably different about gay boys; their differences certainly do not mean they are immoral or wrong.*

and violations from peers. Gay boys cannot necessarily depend on consistent, adequate protective support from teachers and staff or a "more tolerant climate."[8]

Gay boys feel uneasy and awkward when they are indoctrinated and lured into a process where they compare themselves to their straight male peers or sense that they are being judged by and compared to others. Not all gay boys are inclined to be on the sensitive side, but some definitely are more emotionally vulnerable than straight boys. Some gay boys do have less traditionally masculine interests, traits, and features; these differ from the mainstream expectation of standardized straight-normal behaviors and interests from all boys, regardless of whether they are straight or not.

Many gay boys make valiant attempts to forcefully act and be straight enough and *normal* enough by someone else's definition; they overcompensate by seeking approval and a fleeting sense of safety through people-pleasing.

CRITICAL THINKING CHOICE CHECKPOINT #2

Dimension #2 during childhood usually pertains to school environments. Dimension #2 is layered over family influences in Dimension #1. Both school and home are sources of blocking and subjugation, leaving many gay boys feeling inferior to straight boys.

Teachers Set the Tone

School is where gay boys discover how they are perceived outside their family and what happens when their gayness or differentness is more noticeable; this reinforces a sense of urgency and pattern of approval-seeking and limit-testing for gay boys. Schools today may be more aware about LGBTQ+ students or attempt or claim to be affirmative in theory, but the reality is that the generalized concept of normal is still defined as something gay boys are *not*.

Many gay boys do not fully comprehend, officially reveal, or confirm their gayness at younger ages. It is nearly impossible for gay boys to be functionally validated because the system caters to the majority, which will not significantly change. Even gay boys who are clearer about their gayness at a younger age will still likely be apprehensive to reveal their gayness, regardless of an affirmative, less judgmental environment.

Teachers and educational institutions are highly influential. Similar and parallel to the framework of parents and family, educational institutions and teachers have generally operated under a presumption that all students are straight-normal. Today, it is less common that teachers and school settings are as *explicitly* anti-gay; however, similar to the response of parents in Dimension #1, they may never be adequately equipped to acknowledge and validate gay boys as normal.

Negative Messages from the External Environment

Gay boys commonly collude in the blocking effort by hiding their gayness to avoid attention. Similar to most children, they yearn to be liked and approved of by their peers and teachers.

In Dimension #2, after increased social exposure to peers, gay boys become more inquisitive about their own masculinity and value. They learn that being perceived as normal can potentially provide a sense of security, safety, and sometimes supremacy compared to other gay boys who may be experiencing more overt and aggressive anti-gay harassment.

Many gay boys decide that it is safer to avoid or minimize the prospects for being harassed and encroached upon. Gay boys tend to be directly targeted; many will overhear recurring, threatening, hateful inferences about gay-related characteristics. Besides the cutting, vile, and derogatory label of *faggot,* it was somewhat routine to hear references "in the air" that something or *someone* disgusting, stupid, or undesirable is "so gay."

CHAPTER 3

Being Blocked in Adolescence Causes Various Reactions

Adolescence is a developmental stage when most children transition from childhood to adulthood. It can be a notoriously erratic and challenging period when teens become more cognizant of their sexual identity. Prior to adolescence, younger gay boys may contemplate varying degrees of a perplexing presence of same-sex attraction.

With the onset of puberty, gay boys' attraction to other boys is greatly increased. This is an extremely distressing time because the potential for same-sex attraction is more pronounced. The powerful, exciting, more intense homosexual urges also feel more convoluted because of a discouraging, underlying pressure and coercion to avoid embracing natural homosexual urges and feelings.

Adolescent Gay Boys Repress and Compare Themselves to Straight Boys

Despite the awareness of same-sex attraction, the sexual identity of many gay teens remains repressed and/or undetected. Many continue to deliberately block their gayness internally, irrespective of their more intense sexual awakening. As curious and longing for a same-sex outlet as they might be, most gay teens avoid attention that would reveal their private secret. They are conflicted with intense sexual urges like any teen, but their urges are recurrently restricted.

Gay adolescent boys, in particular, actively compare themselves to other boys, most of whom are straight and dissimilar to them. The comparison process contributes to a greater sense of inadequacy. Adolescents are typically hyperfocused on sex. This often also includes a hypersensitivity to gay "indicators" or more effeminate traits and features; the increased exposure can exacerbate hateful, aggressive actions toward gay peers, especially those appearing more stereotypically gay.

Identity Versus Role Confusion

Psychoanalyst and Professor Erik Erikson noted Eight Stages of Psychosocial Development to identify issues that peak during various age ranges. Critical milestones can vary from functional to dysfunctional. The fifth stage, referencing the onset of puberty and adolescence, is called Identity vs. Role Confusion.[9] This is particularly relevant for gay adolescents, who are targets of external pressure and are bound to be in the dysfunctional end of this scope, hence the relativity of the generalized term *role confusion*.

> **CRITICAL THINKING CHOICE CHECKPOINT #3**
>
> Gay boys are commonly encroached upon by parents and school settings because their gayness is often overtly and covertly deterred. This contributes to the blocking of their true selves. Remember, it is the parents, family, school, or similar influences that impact and challenge innate, biologically based homosexuality that causes much of the confusion! In other words, gay boys are made to feel confused; otherwise, they may not have been "confused" at all.

No Confusion About the Confusion

Gay adolescents generally do not instigate the influence of identity confusion; the confusion is caused by external environments not accepting them. The confusion is intensified when gay male teens, like all adolescents, become highly aware of their sexuality; yet gay adolescents have also been indoctrinated to believe that they are supposed to act and be straight-normal.

Different Realities for Different Sexualities: Straight Versus Gay

While it is not encouraged, minors do engage in sexual exploration with other adolescent peers. Teenagers are apt to push the sexual envelope of discovering and experimenting. Straight male adolescents enjoy the freedom to release their supercharged hormonal energy by engaging in sexual exploration with female peers. Compared to a gay peer, straight male adolescents will feel more comfortable to freely express their interest since it is perceived as normal to be attracted to the opposite sex.

If straight boys choose to not (yet) explore sexual relationships with female peers, their choice doesn't carry the same connotation or pose a problem. Many gay teens are understandably fearful and apprehensive about expressing their same-sex attraction. Straight teens have a normalized choice to date, flirt, and experiment if and when they are ready and in a way that feels natural and appropriate to them. Straight teens will not be judged in a comparable way, or ridiculed for acting on their normal adolescent urges, whereas gay teens tend to be penalized and humiliated, if not personally alarmed, by their own natural attraction to the same sex.

> *Gay teens tend to be penalized and humiliated, if not personally alarmed, by their own natural attraction to the same sex.*

Most straight teenage boys have a socially sanctioned opportunity to flirt and date whenever they are ready, able, and interested. Gay boys technically have the same choice or option to explore their attraction to other boys but are often hesitant and deterred to act on this risky, daring move that will likely be judged more harshly. Acting on their attraction can result in demeaning rejection, social humiliation, shaming, and sometimes emotional, verbal, and physically assaultive reactions from their peers.

Gay It Down: Keeping Matters "Less Gay" Also Represses Gay Teens

Many gay male adolescents have been conditioned through years of prior and present blocking that being openly gay will subject them to intense negative scrutiny. Whether they experience absolute or partial clarity about their sexual orientation, many will hesitate or avoid acting on their feelings through repression and blocking. Some avoid dating and more openly expressed sexual interest altogether while others act straight, feigning some forced romantic/sexual interest in dating and connecting with females. Although they are more aware of their homosexual urges, some gay teens predictably want to fit in and be perceived as straight-normal; they may fear consequences of coming out or hope that their strong gay urges will somehow subside. More frustration is likely to build as the homosexual urges become increasingly apparent while the perceived pressure to avoid acknowledging or responding concurrently persists.

Gay adolescents face a challenging undertaking regardless of how open they choose to be about their sexuality. If they are repressed but projecting a straight male persona, the façade takes its toll emotionally and psychologically. This can leave gay teens feeling distressed, resentful, angry, and even more encroached upon and ashamed. If gay teens present in a more neutral capacity, such as not dating or flirting at all, they attempt to avoid the issue as much as possible. They deliberately fail to address their sexuality in any particular way and do not even remotely meet their needs. This puts them essentially in the closet, functioning in a covert operation and, again, placing their authenticity on hold for the benefit of someone else.

Some gay boys are unwilling or less able to successfully block out the reality that their version of normal is profoundly different from their straight peers. Openly gay adolescents should be commended for their braveness; however, in terms of respect and validation, they will likely experience a mixed reception at best from peers, parents, family, and other influential adult figures. Gay boys who come out during adolescence might be seeking self-respect and some sense of relief by being authentic. They rightfully deserve this respect; still, they are bound to be criticized, discouraged, rejected, or punished, even if some peers, parents, and teachers choose to be more respectful, accepting, and understanding.

CHAOTIC MENTAL CHATTER: FROM ANGER TO ANXIETY

Gay adolescents have disturbing, exciting, frightening, and confusing thoughts, feelings, and existential assessment as they navigate their awakening sexuality. They ponder various emotions, awareness, and questions, such as:

- Strong feelings of sexual attraction to other boys

- Generalized and anticipatory anxiety about the future

- Feeling scared and alarmed, yet intrigued to engage in desires thought by some to be deviant and taboo

- Wondering if they are just confused and if these feelings and urges will go away; they question how they will be able to handle the pressure and the consequences of being different if and when they come out

CHAPTER 4

Invalidation and Shame Magnification Are the Cause and Consequence of Being Blocked

Validation is a way someone or something is acknowledged and unconditionally accepted in its present state, with minimal critical, indifferent, opinionated influence, intrusion, or value judgment by someone or something else. The American Psychological Association (APA) defines *validation* as "the process of establishing the truth or logical cogency of something. An example is determining the accuracy of a research instrument in measuring what it is designed to measure."[10]

Shame creates severe humiliation, which can lead to low self-worth, self-loathing, underachieving, and dysfunctional relationships. Shame functions as a mechanism to block gay boys from their gayness. The APA defines *shame* as "a highly unpleasant self-conscious emotion arising from the sense of there being something dishonorable, immodest, or indecorous in one's own conduct or circumstances." Shame is typically characterized by withdrawal from social interaction—for example, by hiding or distracting the attention of another from one's *shameful* action—which can have a profound effect on psychological adjustment and interpersonal relationships. Shame may perpetuate not only avoidant behavior but also defensive, retaliative anger.[11]

Deficient Validation Leads to Insecurity

Much of the perplexity of a developing gay man's self-identity begins in childhood and centers around the disparity between who the gay boy is and who or what their environment expects them to be. Most straight children are validated for who they are, at least on a basic level. However, this does not apply to many gay boys.

Despite improvements in the general reception of homosexuality in society, most gay boys will be fundamentally invalidated. The homosexual orientation of young gay boys is often not entirely clarified yet. Regardless, when gay boys are treated as if they are, will be, or *should* be straight, they are inherently invalidated and blocked. Gay boys are commonly subjected to critical, negative scrutiny instead of authentic validation, which is remarkably different from the average life interactions of straight boys. Beyond the basic invalidation of being groomed to be straight when they're not, negative reinforcement stemming from anti-gay sentiment is also exceedingly invalidating.

> *Much of the perplexity of a developing gay man's self-identity begins in childhood and centers around the disparity between who the gay boy is and who or what their environment expects them to be.*

Feeling deficient validation can bring about shame, fear, and anxiety. Many gay boys respond to deficient validation with an insecure self-image. Invalidation leads to a decreased sense of emotional safety. External invalidation experiences in Dimensions #1 and #2 are likely to persist regardless of how internally aware gay boys are or how well they try to combat and deflect sometimes pervasive invalidation.

The most affirming parents with the best intentions may still be incapable of adequately validating their gay son. Some parents of gay boys are more aware of their son's identity. They may choose to be unconditionally supportive and gay affirmative to the best of their abilities Supportive parents, in this example, will not automatically presume or expect that all children are or should be molded to be straight-normal. Most parents of gay boys will not be undeniably aware of their son's sexual orientation, or worse than that, they will resist acknowledging the gayness if they are aware. It is a tremendous reality to accept for parents and gay boys.

> ### CRITICAL THINKING CHOICE CHECKPOINT #4
>
> Gay boys are generally validated for being something they are not. In their search for proper validation, many feel they must repress who they are. Therefore, gay boys are essentially validated when they are *not* being their true selves. Gay boys are challenged with this double bind at a very young age. Some become self-loathing people-pleasers, a tendency that often persists into adulthood, and others become abnormally narcissistic.

Heteronormative conditioning is a reinforcement that promotes heterosexual orientation as the preferred or "normal" option; it is a major component of the framework by which mainstream society operates. Gay boys cannot be validated when their gayness is essentially *invisible*. Comments, references, negative criticisms about gay men, and modeled behaviors remind gay boys that it is more normal to be straight. Redirecting gay tendencies is even more relevant during adolescence, when gay boys are often verbally or physically besieged about what will happen to them if they are a "faggot." Many gay adolescents internalize these threatening, hateful attacks as reminders to *hate themselves*.

Gay Boys Assume, "You're Not Going to Understand Me Anyway, So I Can't Win."

This hopeless, cynical thought process may continue further with some version of "If you do somewhat understand me, you may not approve of or like me, and it may not make any difference." As they mature through their childhood and adolescent stages, gay boys become more cognizant about the lacking validation. Gay teens assume they will not be adequately understood, whether they are officially labeled and correctly identified as gay or not. Many are deliberately hiding anyway, so gay boys also figure that other people, including their parents and family at times, won't know who they really are, or worse, they feel strongly that they won't be liked and could suffer dire consequences if the truth is discovered. Gay boys may then respond by blocking others, because of lacking trust, including family and various potentially close relationships; this is a systemic cycle, sometimes lingering into adulthood, that may also eventually block out other gay men, causing disconnection and invalidation.

Various Degrees of Validation Equate to Various Degrees of Being Blocked

Invalidation for gay boys can be thought of as a **continuum**; the impact of validation can both cause and *be* caused by being blocked from their true gay selves. Many gay men learn to block themselves from being especially intimate and trusting others, including other gay men.

There are several degrees of validation or lack thereof. Some gay boys are exposed to **aggressive invalidation**. In this case, they can be subjected to a range of potentially excessive, anti-gay, vile, and aggressively hateful threats. Aggressive invalidation sometimes occurs in fundamentalist/extremist families that are markedly clear about their negative, critical stance on homosexuality. Any gay indicators from their (gay) son will be adversely received.

A higher level of validation requires well-informed, gay-affirmative parents as well as gay-affirming outside sources.

Perhaps a more common experience for gay boys on a validation continuum occurs where they are at a midpoint and may feel a sense of what I refer to as **validation-neutral.** This appears to reflect a "don't ask/don't tell" policy. It implies that gay boys are not being egregiously or overtly abused or harassed, but they are also not acknowledged for who they are; they are still essentially blocked at home and school, despite the absence of intense, outwardly hateful anti-gay treatment. On the surface, gay boys in this predicament appear to experience less harsh cruelty and damage because they are not necessarily targeted in a blatant and hateful way, yet they are not particularly well validated either. Validation-neutral is a state where gay boys are somewhat ignored in terms of any deep sense of acknowledgment. However, neutrality still renders this level significantly lacking in adequate, normal, healthy validation.

The Effects of Various Validation Levels

A classic example of validation-neutral occurs in families that fail to address and acknowledge their son's gayness or much about sexuality in general. Family members tend to be avoidant despite indicators from their son that he may be gay; they are also less likely to express or encourage feelings and emotions. Parents or teachers may be averse to discussing or referencing deeper feelings or conversations about LGBTQ+ matters. Even if teachers, parental figures, and influential adults are more flexible or open about these matters, the gay boys themselves often feel awkward, scared, or embarrassed and avoid having an exposed, sometimes self-incriminating conversation about their gayness. For example, if a parent or teacher came right out and asked or respectfully confronted their son or student about being gay, he may deny it.

The **neutrality** is still invalidating because the gay boy is not acknowledged and affirmed for who he really is, with the gayness ultimately unaddressed. Neutrality may seem more desirable to gay adolescents, even if it means partially blocking, repressing, and avoiding any indicators that reflect their gayness. The alternative may consist of a high potential for an incendiary response from parents or peers if gayness is revealed or confirmed by the gay boy himself (if he comes out and identifies as gay of his own accord, is less able to hide or repress it, or is maliciously "outed" by others somehow).

An example of validation-neutral in the school setting is the more reserved (closeted) gay boy who can also quietly pass for straight. He is less likely to experience overt, hate-filled bullying. However, not being overtly gay-bashed doesn't effectively make the gay adolescent any less gay, positively acknowledged, or safe about who he really is. Validation-neutrality is conditional and somewhat passive-aggressive; the external responses may not be obviously damaging, but they also do not foster a sense of normal validation.

A small number of gay boys experience a healthy level of validation. A **highly validating** position is less common for gay boys because of the infrequent presence of a necessary and delicate balance of factors. A higher level of validation requires well-informed, gay-affirmative parents as well as gay-affirming outside sources, like school, teachers, officials, and perhaps, a more progressive community/location (such as a more liberal city, state, or region).

Highly gay-affirmative parents, guardians, or similarly influential mentors/figures are more aware and don't automatically assume that all children are heterosexual by default; this is somewhat rare. High levels of validation require unconditional acceptance and involve a unique level of understanding and a shame-free ability to support a gay son. Another critical component of higher validation also requires that the gay boy himself is likely more aware, receptive, comfortable, open, and willing or perhaps is already "out" about his sexuality, even at a younger age.

Trailblazing Self-Validation

A small number of gay boys will refuse to easily accommodate their family's expectations that they are straight-normal and less "defiant"; they occasionally find an opportunity to speak up. The backlash from an invalidating environment can create more conflict, with power struggles likely to ensue as some parents try to repress and combat the gay boy's gayness. This type of family attempts to block any kind of noncompliance with straight-normal traits and behaviors. The tension and extreme views of a non-gay-affirming, hateful family sometimes provoke the gay boy to act out and rebel a bit more rather than block himself. Some gay boys are also more fearless and may choose to come out in their school setting and face the potential consequences and reactions from peers and teachers.

Shame, Shame, We Know Your Name: How Shameful Feelings Become Magnified

Shame is an unpleasant, self-conscious emotion associated with deficient validation. Feeling a sense of shame directly impedes a positive sense of self-worth. Shame is a powerful, insidious part of the development of most gay boys. If a child is being properly and reasonably validated, they are less likely to feel a sense of shame.

Gay boys are more likely than straight boys to receive relentless criticism; they often feel singled out, overlooked, underacknowledged, dismissed, and devalued. When gay boys feel ashamed about a multitude of issues, they become hypersensitive to being repeatedly shamed. Smaller, less problematic matters can become *magnified*. This creates hyperawareness and a sense of insecurity about their self-worth as they may experience a perpetual underlying state of feeling disgraced for their gayness.

A transference effect triggers these emotionally charged situations. Each time they feel the familiar sense of shame for one matter, comment, criticism, or incident, it is often emotionally associated with, connected to, and intensified by other shaming experiences. Because of this transference, the systemic sense of shame can be exacerbated and triggered by a variety of even slightly unsettling, distrusting incidents and scenarios.

Gay boys commonly harbor a sense of shame early in childhood because they are often made to feel penetrating self-loathing.[12] Even moderately shameful experiences can become reinterpreted and more intensely internalized or magnified. Eventually, some gay boys may feel as though they deserve to be shamed; therefore, they will sometimes act out, seeking negative attention, for example, and then create additional shaming conditions for themselves.

Less Aware, Insensitive Parents and Teachers Facilitate and Trigger Shame Magnification

Despite recent improvements in LGBTQ+ tolerance, parents and teachers are still likely to be less aware or prepared to understand the full scope of the developmental struggles that often transpire privately for many gay boys. Shame magnification can be thought of as systemic hypersensitivity to anything that feels familiar to shame; it is an activated "trigger receptor." Any child might be vulnerable to shaming incidents, but the shame baseline is already well engrained in gay boys.

Shame magnification occurs when gay boys are insensitively and unnecessarily judged and criticized for petty concerns that any child technically could be confronted about. This may include imprudent, random events, such as when parents or teachers hassle them or "pick" on them about essentially minor behavioral traits or actions that could also be dealt with more constructively or ignored. Parents and teachers commonly miss the mark and have no idea how troubled their gay son or student is when they make an issue out of minor, petty matters. Recall the double-bind: If they were to theoretically confront the situation and ask, "What is going on with you?" the gay boy will more than likely answer emphatically, "Nothing, I'm fine." The reality is that many gay boys feel overly blocked and likely too terrified to reveal their shameful secret; in fact, they don't feel "fine" at all.

The most hostile example of shaming endured by gay boys includes the shockingly common attacks of being referred to in a derogatory manner, like being repeatedly called anti-gay slurs such as *faggot*.

The more outrageous hateful attacks and discrimination, which may not always include overt, inflammatory slurs, are mainly from ignorant, nasty peers, but they also might originate from adults, like teachers, parents, family members, coaches, mentors, or supposedly trusted persons of authority. Perhaps there has been some improvement here in recent decades. However, fellow students/peers are still likely to engage in verbally or physically abusive anti-gay comments and attacks. So being additionally shamed in various ignorant, petty ways is the last thing gay boys need, but it can be a common, yet damaging, experience. Shame magnification is bound to occur unless gay boys are more fortunate to experience less shame or are more capable of deflecting a sense of shame in general.

Shaming incidents feel like threats and challenges to a gay boy's already fractured self-awareness and self-assuredness.

Shaming incidents feel like threats and challenges to a gay boy's already fractured self-awareness and self-assuredness. Think about this scenario: Instead of feeling positive and validated, many gay boys grow up feeling pessimistic, passive, and powerless. Consequently, they often lack assertiveness and have difficulty getting their genuine needs met. If gay boys attempt to affirm themselves and refute negative, toxic attacks, they run a high likelihood of being demoralized again. Being repeatedly blocked does not stack the odds in their favor.

Environments outside the family also tend to fail gay boys, many of whom are essentially closeted. They lack full awareness or the capability to understand their gayness or are not yet openly accepting and identifying as gay. Parents, teachers, and similar authority figures may reinforce the notion that the gay boy is damaged and defective without fully acknowledging who he is or what the core issue might be. Furthermore, if there is any acknowledgment of him maybe being *gay-ish*, the feedback he receives is mostly negative or candidly anti-gay. Some gay boys will be criticized for being too "soft" or girly, for whining or lisping, and for not being tough, masculine, or *normal* like the "normal" that applies to heterosexual boys. Some gay boys will continue to distort reality in a similar fashion and sustain and embrace the interpreted messages. Tragically, some gay boys begin to believe they actually are inferior and should "know their place."

Environments outside the family tend to fail gay boys, many of whom are essentially closeted and not completely aware or understanding of their gayness.

SHAME MAGNIFICATION

Gay boys are subjected to shame magnification caused by unsettling anxiety, which can perpetuate chronic shame and anticipatory anxiety. Some examples include:

» **Being easily hurt or overly sensitive,** offended, or conflict-avoidant. Negative feedback, bad news, bad reviews, rumors, threats, or criticism can be magnified;

» **Having chronic self-doubt and lacking self-confidence:** being hypercritical and quick to self-blame and self-condemn;

» **Acting out and seeking negative attention,** and having poor, "fluid" boundaries perpetuates additional shaming;

» **Deliberately sabotaging or creating a "self-fulfilling prophecy,"** feeling shameful and disgusting, and embracing those feelings to live up to the shame;

» **Being drawn to unhealthy, dysfunctional relationships:** people-pleasing, codependency, and accommodating others;

» **Misperceiving and minimizing a need for basic respect and acknowledgment** from others;

» **Being a bully, sometimes targeting other gay boys** or more vulnerable peers, acting passive-aggressive, jealous, envious, and hateful;

» **Displaying symptoms of characterological issues/personality disorders,** caused from excessive invalidation and chronic shame magnification (read more in Part IV).

PART II

Blocking in the Adult Gay Male Community (GMC)

CHAPTER 5

Dimension #3: The Adult Gay Male Community (GMC)

The gay male community (GMC) is a place where gay men regularly seek camaraderie and connection. It is a safe space that proposes to normalize gayness in men. Yet, in some ways, the GMC can also function like an immature adult high school zone. Gay men in the GMC initially assume they will experience a sense of love, support, tolerance, and validation. After experiencing a frequently turbulent, ostracizing childhood, many presume that the GMC will provide a sense of tolerance and acceptance amid an implied challenge to maintain individuality. However, some gay men soon learn their experience with and around the GMC also includes elements of unfriendliness, rejection, *in*validation, judging, and blocking.

> *Some gay men soon learn their experience with and around the GMC also includes elements of unfriendliness, rejection, invalidation, judging, and blocking.*

The presence and pressure of mainstream social norms within the GMC challenge gay men to separate from those collective norms in exchange for a sense of personal, unblocked, evolving happiness. This contradiction poses a confusing quagmire of gay-affirming acceptance; ironically, the dynamics in the GMC can include homophobic subtleties and nasty value judgments from and among gay men in the GMC.

As gay men enter some version of Dimension #3 of the GMC,

they anticipate *not* being blocked or needing to block themselves from others. However, a perplexing situation develops instead, where they may now feel blocked by other gay men. In childhood, many gay men only experience limited normalized group-identity support from other gay male peers, who are also repressed, avoidant, and blocked. Non-gay-affirming messages during childhood reinforce the idea that straight-normal is more desirable; some gay men bring forth a history of feeling abnormal, thus continuing an adult version of blocking within the GMC.

> *Non-gay-affirming messages during childhood reinforce the idea that straight-normal is more desirable.*

Big Gay Dreams and Partially Realized Hope After Years of Being Blocked in Dimensions #1 and #2

Blocking in Dimension #3 is an ironic third layer that is sometimes a bizarre culmination of the previous years of being blocked in Dimensions #1 and #2. Young gay men learn there is increased support from connecting with like-minded individuals, but there is also disappointment. They later must learn to navigate a different type of blocking that specifically pertains to gay men in the GMC. The new challenges stem from interactions with other gay men who have also internalized a history of blocking from their youth.

In theory, the GMC has potential for a sense of belonging and "community," but this kind of idealistic camaraderie is not so immediately accessible without learning the dynamics of the GMC. Many gay men must confront a rigid hierarchy and a different protocol of norms to decipher in the GMC, despite their presumption that they can be "out and proud."

> *Young gay men learn there is increased support from connecting with like-minded individuals, but there is also disappointment.*

> **CRITICAL THINKING CHOICE CHECKPOINT #5**
>
> Gay men will potentially interact with other equally challenged gay men who are also recovering from a history of being blocked in childhood. This manifests as damaged, inexperienced gay men joining with one another.

Some of the dynamics of Dimension #3 include an array of passive-aggressive head games, such as sending mixed messages and engaging in high school–like social climbing; some grow through this process while others do not. They must figure out how to navigate and deflect these disagreeable effects in the GMC.

The Blocking Dynamic Prevalent in the GMC Appears in Several Ways and for Numerous Reasons

1. Guarded Self-Protection

Childhood blocking served as a protective function for some gay men; many reenact this pattern of heightened caution that undermines connections as adults in the GMC. Separating from earlier childhood blocking experiences continues to be a struggle for some.

Earlier indoctrination of hiding, lying, or blocking becomes ingrained. The lack of gay affirmation in Dimensions #1 or #2 hinder normal childhood psychosexual and psychosocial development. Some gay men enter the GMC socially and sexually hindered and less emotionally stable; they may be slow to learn and accept that they don't need to people-please and define themselves by external approval, *and they never needed to in the first place.*

> *Childhood blocking served as a protective function for some gay men; many reenact this pattern ... that undermines connections as adults in the GMC.*

2. Collective Social Climbing

Blocking and being guarded or aloof is part of a social norm in the GMC that is modeled and reinforced through the influence of mainstream gay attitudes, temperaments, and values. Some in the GMC will mimic a learned, pretentious, defensive, and elitist attitude. This counterproductive behavior is ultimately blocking and complicates efforts for achieving healthy self-respect and successful relationships.

3. Upgrading

Some gay men fall into a habit of waiting for someone better to come along. It is as though they are scouting for potential upgrading opportunities; this frequently includes posturing, arrogant snobbery, and rejection of other gay men. This dismissive behavior may continue beyond the earlier coming-out stages of their twenties. Some gay men see this superficiality as acceptable, and may adopt a defensive, elitist persona that perpetuates the blocking effect.

4. Fear of Intimacy = Fear of Gayness

Some gay men have a need for self-protection because they fear intimacy, which I believe is ultimately and primarily a fear of embracing their gayness. These fears of commitment are often driven by internalized homophobia, immaturity, and a persistent need for external approval. Emotional delay is common among gay men; for example, a 21-year-old gay man might have the emotional responses of an adolescent.

Displaying an arrogant, cocky attitude or having rigid aesthetic requirements is an effective way to circumvent facing one's gayness. This avoidance is reminiscent of childhood, when some felt pressured to block others because they were being or feeling subjugated by their parents and peers for *being* gay.

The constraints from childhood that block the option to be freely gay theoretically should have dissipated. However, the fear and anxiety of being in a gay relationship, or even exploring their sexuality, may suppress some gay men. Others will opt to be inebriated on drugs or alcohol to lower their inhibitions and feel more comfortable to flirt and engage in gay sex or anonymous, noncommitted sexual rendezvous.

Not every gay man will have the same complicated experiences or afflictions as the aforementioned. However, if they don't personally struggle with intimacy fears, they will likely meet some other gay men who do and who will block them.

5. Consequences of FOMO (Fear of Missing Out)

Seeking perfection limits opportunities, creates a "disposable people" mentality, and dismisses viable options. Gay men who fear they are missing a better option may feel stress or anxiety and block other gay men. Seeking adherence to stringent criteria inevitably causes a chronic cycle of feeling things are "never good enough." Note that this is quite a departure from a young gay male's previous experiences while being mostly closeted and navigating a straight world.

During their childhoods, gay men commonly do not have viable choices to date or sexually explore with. Most gay boys are either repressed or are secretly sneaking around, similar to what closeted adult gay men sometimes do; this is also referred to as "on the down-low" or DL. For adult gay men today, there are more choices and additional social acceptance, and there is less need to be on the DL. Some gay men still fear a punitive response to revealing their true gayness, so they may choose to be more discreet or remain on the DL.

Some gay men who are seeking gay connections will dismiss unwanted relationships they feel are deficient or are no longer needed. They may be mimicking a perceived social norm in the GMC to upgrade, obtain, or comply with more stringent perfectionistic standards; this can pertain to dates, mates, even friends, and particularly to

> *During their childhoods, gay men commonly do not have viable choices to date or sexually explore with.*

casual encounters or those that don't quite measure up to expectations.

This is a *disposable people* mentality that rationalizes cutting off relationships. Some gay men are triggered with homophobic feelings, or they contrive a grandiose excuse that the other man is not good enough. Other times, a gay man desires variety, so he disposes of the current gay man in his life. This may mean a relationship is terminated with little or no explanation; other times, a gay man is rapidly dismissed after a date or hookup. Engaging in arbitrary relationship dynamics is not conducive to developing healthy intimacy.

Anti-Gay Bias, Discrimination, Hate, Homophobia, Ignorance, and Value Judgments

Many gay men report being subjected to various sources of discrimination. As adults, they are potentially more connected to a gay community, yet they may also contend with increased overt homophobia since they are more visible and openly gay. Even though they are now adults and more apt to explore their sexuality, the potential for experiencing a negative response from parts of society still exists. Millions of older gay men incurred much worse default, standardized anti-gay bias and discrimination in previous generations. As more gay men choose to come out of the closet, society is increasingly familiar with gay men; even with that familiarity, some other parts of mainstream (straight) society continue to object to homosexuality.

Gay men either block themselves from others because it is a familiar process until they know better or because they are scared and anxious. When observing the behavior of fellow insecure, inexperienced, damaged gay men, some may conclude that being aloof and avoidantly blocking out gay men is acceptable. Alternatively, gay men may also be on the receiving end of being blocked by other gay men when they find themselves pointlessly trying to connect with unavailable, dysfunctional options. Some gay men become disgusted with the dissolution and perpetual disappointment.

CRITICAL THINKING CHOICE CHECKPOINT #6

Individual gay men can potentially create a collective impact on social norms in the GMC. The bottom line is that gay men in the GMC will deal with blocking that stems from either their own experiences or someone else's. Many almost subconsciously participate in blocking themselves, beginning in childhood, after being conditioned to do so. Even into adulthood, gay men are frequently victims of blocking in and out of the GMC and, conversely, will block others as well as themselves.

CHAPTER 6

The M-Ranking® Search for Male Perfection Creates Cutthroat Judging and Blocking in the GMC

> **CLARIFYING A FEW THINGS
> ABOUT BEING GAY *OR* STRAIGHT**
>
> Some people are born gay, and most others are born straight. Some of those who are gay choose to be more revealing about their sexuality than others. Some are more obviously or stereotypically gay, eccentric, or effeminate than others. Some will have a harder time than others with self-acceptance and the coming-out and unblocking process. Gay men commonly have to overcome the lingering effects of childhood trauma to improve trust and intimacy as adults.
>
> » Being gay or straight, in or out of the closet, is not wrong or bad.
> » Being a gay man who is masculine, feminine, gay, straight-acting, or straight-passing is not wrong or bad.
> » Being more or less effeminate or more or less openly gay is not wrong or bad.
> » Being troubled and suffering emotional and psychological damage from struggling with self-acceptance as a gay boy or gay man are tragic and unfortunate.

The Power Position of a High M-Ranking: The 5 Ms of Male Perfection

Some gay men apply a highly judgmental rationale when assessing themselves and others. I have defined superficial idealized male perfection in this discussion as the **M-Ranking,** which describes a concept and rating system comprised of five distinct categories. Together, they form the primary **5 Ms.** These criteria dominate the aggregate value of the M-Ranking assessment in the GMC.

Collectively, they are a construct and a composite group of criteria that function as part of one social dynamic in the GMC. M-Ranking serves as a rating scale that can be predictably, potentially, universally, subtly, or actively used by any gay man at any point to superficially judge, assess, and rate themselves and other gay men.

> **THE PRIMARY 5 MS OF M-RANKING**
>
> [M1] Masculinity
>
> [M2] Manhood (endowment)
>
> [M3] Model looks and muscles
>
> [M4] Money and materialism
>
> [M5] Mainstream appeal

M1 *Masculinity*

A primary value of the 5 Ms of the M-Ranking System is *masculinity* and an implied higher ability to pass for straight. This rating process includes rigorously judging the manliness and various superficial aesthetic qualities of other gay men; it is sometimes a manifestation of underlying self-loathing and criticism of gayness.[13] Masculinity and male perfection have become highly regarded by gay men and a comprehensive summary or reflection of the other portions of the M-Ranking. While coming out as an adult and reclaiming some degree of a gay male identity, ironically, some gay men become preoccupied with presenting and being perceived as more stereotypically heterosexual. Regardless of their actual demeanor, a large segment of gay men tend to perceive masculinity and qualities of acting or appearing "less gay," also known as "straight-acting," to be of crucial importance.

M2 *Manhood*

Penis size, sexual performance, virility, sexual desirability, and sex appeal are immensely valued by gay men. Penis size is associated with a power position for many gay men; it includes a masculine identification with a fantasy of being well-endowed, "hung," or having, obtaining, and being intimate with a mate who is well-endowed.

Some gay men conclude that a larger endowment will make them feel superior and more of a man than other gay men. They may also presume that other gay men perceive average or smaller endowments as unattractive, powerless, feminine, soft, weak, and not masculine or manly enough.

M3 *Model Looks and Muscles*

Physical strength and having an above-average, muscular, lean, athletic, or jock or gym-body physique are highly valued by gay men of all ages. Model looks also include a generally higher-than-average overall physical aesthetic appearance; achieving this phenomenal caliber of physical beauty is a cherished ideal, coupled with stunning facial features that may be equivalent to that of a professional model.

M4 *Money and Materialism*

Power and connections may indicate status and, thus, a higher desirability. The trappings of materialism include luxurious cars, homes, clothes, lavish vacations, and sometimes sex workers or escorts. Money may be used in conjunction with material items and offers a means to essentially purchase a way into various situations as an alternate or last resort; money and materials may be used to compete or compensate for other aesthetic deficiencies, including being or feeling less attractive and fit, less masculine, less youthful, or having a smaller endowment.

M5 *Mainstream Appeal*

The ability to broadly and successfully blend in with both gay and straight environments and communities is an appealing trait in the GMC. This is more than just good looks or being straight-acting or straight-passing. Mainstream appeal also includes a favorable, above-average attribute of popularity, charisma, and likability, reminiscent of a high school– or adolescent-like stage of development and social norms where there is popularity competition.

Perceptions of M-Ranking in the GMC

You've Been Blocked assumes that many gay men are prone to engage in or be affected by the pursuit of the perfect M-Ranking during at least one time period of their adult lives. Although not every gay man succumbs to the influence of the standard M-Ranking process, the impact of the pursuit of perfection in the GMC is considerable.

Some gay men perceive the concept of M-Ranking as a well-established, acceptable, desirable, and logical behavioral social norm. Other gay men in the GMC may not be consumed by the M-Ranking, yet at one point or another, they will engage with those who are more supportive of this philosophy. There are also gay men who consciously reject the M-Ranking approach and don't subscribe to this philosophy.

M-Ranking variables are still only a subjective assessment; they do not need to be such an influential social norm. The M-Ranking value system is normalized if gay men willfully choose it. Gay men can opt to define their own priorities rather than adhere to what some perceive to be a collective, systemic valuation in the GMC.

One would think the combination and emphasis placed on the superficiality of the M-Ranking variables would render them comparatively less important, yet they continue to captivate many gay men at some point. Regardless, deeper, more authentic values pale in comparison for too many gay men, at least for a while, especially in their younger years. Other values include those qualities that facilitate a sense of internal satisfaction, authenticity, intimacy, and longer-term connections. Does anyone in the GMC know "who" is officially authorized to define perfection? The M-Ranking System is an example of GMC-institutionalized conformity that impedes and blocks the development of more authentic, appropriate connections with potential mates.

> **CRITICAL THINKING CHOICE CHECKPOINT #7**
>
> The reality is that more evolved gay men must eventually realize that they will rarely, if ever, obtain a slim margin of male perfection either personally or in another person. Until maturation or more reasonable thought is developed, the pursuit of perfection ignites a potent response. The reactions to this seemingly collective, critical judging in the GMC may include unnecessary competition, feelings of envy, resentment, anger, social climbing, profound inadequacy, classism, and elitism.

What Is Being Pursued in the M-Ranking?

The M-Ranking System of valuation is a likely continuation of earlier distorted thinking that fosters inauthenticity and systemic blocking. Complying with the values of the M-Ranking System is certainly not an obligatory process. This value system provides mostly limited returns based on a contrived, alluring sense of elitism and superior status.

Accommodating Others Is a Learned Behavior from Childhood

Gay men contend with the history of conditioned messages from childhood. In their adulthood, Dimension #3, some gay men continue to wrestle with the idea of presenting their authentic selves. For some, authenticity comes in exchange for an idealized reward they presume might derive from being associated with a strong M-Ranking. In other words, some gay men believe their quest for male perfection and adequate acceptance can finally be achieved if they have a high M-Ranking or at least are associated with other gay men who they perceive as fulfilling the M-Ranking criteria.

Faulty historical messages manipulated gay men in their

childhood to believe that **accommodating others** is more of a priority than meeting their own needs. Hence, they followed suit in blocking their gayness to please everyone else from parents to peers. In Dimension #3, some adult gay men still maintain these inappropriate, degrading, systematically distorted messages or "old tapes" internalized during their childhood. Many gay men initially interpret a new variation of the need to appear acceptable or normal; this is also defined by some other gay men in the GMC as "perfection." Ultimately, they are still operating under the distortion that they must be approved of by others.

In addition to the history of people-pleasing and approval-seeking from their childhood years, some gay men will repurpose the pattern for social climbing in the GMC. In Dimension #3, some will now obsess about seeking approval, like they formerly sought (and still may currently clamor for) from their parents or peers, from other gay men.

The childhood version of perfection-seeking was about achieving acceptance and safety. Tragically, during this process in Dimensions #1 and #2, many gay boys learned their approval "rating" was higher if everything *looked* acceptable, which was also defined by someone else. *Acceptable* was frequently deemed physically appearing and acting straight, masculine, and normal (straight-normal). A sense of safety versus the ominous threats of being shamed and bullied became a strong incentive to "gay it down," even if it meant self-blocking.

Gay men understandably crave a positive, validating response from other gay men. They seek a sense of identity, approval, and acceptance. In the hierarchy of M-Rankings, greater compliance with most or all of the M-Ranking qualities is like an ego boost that gives some gay men a sense of superiority. This judgmental, cutthroat dynamic is similar to adolescent subtleties when gay men felt excluded and blocked for not being straight-normal.

The Illusion of Perfection Invariably Creates Additional Blocking Effects

Some gay men convince themselves that they can achieve this level of perfection in those they seek as well as in themselves. During a gay man's childhood, a similar system was displayed as a vexing course in trying to be straight-normal. As adults in the GMC, gay men might think they are solely seeking perfection for themselves, but the idealization now functions within the collective pecking order framework of the GMC.

Am I Good Enough for the Gay Men of the GMC?

Romanticizing perfection appeals to some impressionable gay men; perhaps they expect an increased sense of power and market value in the GMC. There may always be a following (likely more relative to younger adulthood, but not exclusively) within the GMC that will strongly support the pursuit for perfection-based traits and conditions. Those who determine that pursuing the M-Ranking qualities is unhealthy must challenge the implied pressure to comply with that value system.

Since the perfect version of the M-Ranking is seldom obtainable, maintaining these standards can contribute to a systemic, general blocking effect in the GMC. These expectations interfere with connections and intimacy that may otherwise transpire. Gay men who continue to prioritize compliance with the M-Ranking valuation risk becoming chronically unhappy and unfulfilled.

CHAPTER 7

M-RANKING #1: Masculinity Is the Composite and Core of the M-Ranking System

Males display varying traits of masculinity. It would be ideal if there was less value judgment about gayness or masculinity levels, but this may not significantly change. It is a fair argument that all people should be able to be their natural selves; any gay man should have the option to be attracted to the traits they like.

As children, many gay men grow up observing and idealizing the idea of masculinity as a measurement of stereotypically heterosexual qualities. In large part, the M-Ranking is made up of attributes that some gay men historically learned and associated with being more heterosexual or straight-acting. There is a faction of adult gay men who adamantly self-proclaim that they are considered genuinely masculine; there are some gay men who also feel qualified to assess other gay men to determine whether they're masculine enough.

Internalized homophobia occurs when gay men feel and project a strong sense of fear, discomfort, and self-loathing because of their own gayness; it can impact gay men whether in or out of the closet. The search for a slim margin of perfection is one by-product of internalized homophobia because demanding stringent compliance with these qualities generates limited returns. The M-Ranking's outlier "M" of masculinity in the GMC fulfills a specific and overall perception about presenting and passing more easily for heterosexual/straight.

For some, achieving the status of straight-passing feels more normal and safer and attracts less negative, anti-gay attention.

Some gay men are authentically straighter-acting, traditionally more stereotypically masculine, and also generally comfortable with themselves. However, other gay men feel less secure, and, regardless of their demeanor, must eventually address a sense of discomfort with being gay; this includes fears and hang-ups about possibly being perceived in a negative capacity *because of their gayness* as opposed to their supposed level of masculinity. Many gay men have to confront their own homophobic feelings, regardless of how masculine they or any potential gay man they encounter might be.

> *The M-Ranking is made up of attributes that some gay men historically learned and associated with being more heterosexual or straight-acting.*

Some gay men maintain erroneously learned interpretations that being gay means they are not real men. Less masculine gay boys are more readily identified and less capable of concealing their gayness. Thus, by adulthood, gay men may be even more hyperaware and reactive about the implications of masculinity; some gay men feel pressured to respond to scrutiny about how masculine they actually are versus their own subjective self-perception and definition of masculinity and how masculine they personally *think* they are.

CRITICAL THINKING CHOICE CHECKPOINT #8

The concept and quality of being perceived as straight-acting leads to a greater sense of power for some gay men. Much of the GMC has essentially accepted the concept of masculinity as a euphemism for appointing gay men as either more or less straight-acting. Collectively, the masculinity value judgment in the GMC comes with an association of greater desirability to some extent, thus a higher M-Ranking and a hopeful perception of increased potential popularity.

Heterosexism Links Masculinity Power, Safety, and Being Straight-Normal

Heterosexism promotes the belief that heterosexuality is normal and preferred. Gay men who haven't learned that they can be subjected to this violation may concur with this devaluing belief. Consequently, some are prone to continuing their attempts at toning down their gayness as needed later in adulthood/the GMC.

The history of heterosexualization during their suggestible childhoods manipulated and blocked many gay boys, so some of them developed distorted beliefs that gayness is inferior. It is a heterosexist view to think that being heterosexual is better; however, some gay men continue to abide by this belief.

IDEALIZED CONCLUSIONS ABOUT BEING "MORE MASCULINE"

Some gay men may make the following presumptions about the benefits of masculinity in the GMC:

» There are more advantages to being masculine.

» I will be perceived as more attractive if I am masculine.

» I will be perceived as stronger and more powerful.

» I will be liked more and approved of by both gay and straight people.

» I will be higher up on the hierarchy and have more power in both gay and straight worlds (M-Ranking valuation).

» I will be superior to other gay men and externally perceived to be as good as straight men (people-pleasing).

» I will be happier and have a "better" life.

» I will be in greater control.

Idealizing masculinity as a summation of the M-Ranking is a reminder and a method that entices some gay men to devalue other gay men (and homosexuality in general) in the GMC. This superficial judging is also evident as some younger gay men tend to erupt on social media correspondence, allegedly complaining about the parameters of masculinity and femme-shaming in the GMC.[14]

Predictable exposure to negative, invalidating messages leads some gay men to attribute being less masculine or more gay-appearing to being weak and undesirable.

Idealizing Masculinity and Heterosexuality Perpetuates Non-Gay-Affirmativism

> **Here is one breakdown of a masculinity thought process that prioritizes straight-acting for some gay men.**
>
> » If I'm perceived as too feminine,
> » I will be thought of as (too) gay.
> » Being gay is bad, wrong, undesirable, weak, and unsafe.
> » Being straight is better and safer than being gay.

Some gay men do naturally act, appear, and sound more masculine than others. Being a masculine male is a desirable trait. However, demanding expectations of masculine male *perfection* invalidate authentic identity, particularly if the majority of men do not meet this standard.

Demanding expectations of masculine male perfection invalidate authentic identity.

Some Gay Men Conclude That Homosexuality Is Equal to Femininity

Most gay men are not especially effeminate, but they are not exceptionally masculine either. Most gay men are not genuinely hypermasculine. Unless it is an affected and unnatural uptight posturing, this is typically displayed by less secure, defensive gay men who struggle with their gayness. Despite what is sometimes made out to be satire, most gay men do *not* personify an overtly flamboyant, "queen" stereotype. Generally, however, they do tend to be at least somewhat more effeminate overall as compared to heterosexual men. It would be a fallacy to declare that there is no difference at all in the demeanor between gay and straight men *altogether.* While most gay men assert that they are born homosexual, the biologically based differences compared to straight males are not entirely understood.[15]

> *Most gay men do* not *personify an overtly flamboyant, stereotypical "queen" stereotype.*

There are heterosexual men who are not necessarily the most macho, hyper-male, stereotypically masculine examples either. Almost all males, regardless of sexual orientation, are moderately masculine. Unless they are affected, insecure, homophobic, or ignorant, or they question their own sexuality, most straight men who are secure with their sexual identity do not deliberately posture or exaggerate their masculinity by acting hypermasculine. Gay men will not threaten a straight man who is generally comfortable with his sexual identity. A more evolved, self-aware gay man is also less likely to be threatened or insecure about his own sexuality, including his level of masculinity.

In contrast, men who identify as heterosexual and are also less secure may harbor uneasiness about their own sexual orientation; they are more apt to be uncomfortable with the concept of gay men.[16] Those gay men who are more secure about their sexuality feel less need to block self or others or to be phony.

M-Ranking Qualities May Form a Composite Masculinity Assessment

In a sense, some gay men may perceive or incorrectly equate the M-Ranking to an overgeneralized composite of masculinity. For example, gay men who are regarded as having a higher M-Ranking may be more likely to be perceived as (more) masculine; they may also be seen as more desirable, attractive, "hot," muscular, wealthy, and well-equipped. The reality is that they may not necessarily be remarkably masculine or reflect any or every aspect of the other M-Ranking measurements, nor are they aesthetically perfect.

Is Prioritizing Masculinity as "Just a Preference" a Valid Expectation?

Attraction to different qualities, including physical appearance and a more masculine or feminine demeanor, is a subjective preference that varies from person to person. There is a line between having preferences and maintaining overly rigid demands and expectations born from harsh criticisms and value judgments. In the GMC, gay men's preferences for what they deem acceptable sometimes lead to being blocked and ultimately consumed by their own homophobic or grandiose, strict demands, which will rarely be accommodated.

Some gay men will vehemently maintain that their attraction and staunch search for ultramasculine men is just an innate sexual/physical attraction, which is, of course, their prerogative; they insist their affinity for masculinity is based only on personal preference that is not homophobic or non-gay-affirmative.

The spectrum of preference can become problematic in this case. A preoccupation with the overvaluation of masculinity incentivizes adherence to the M-Ranking. The quest for ideal masculinity influences the perfection-seeking nature of the M-Ranking. These inflexible demands are driven by frequently unobtainable criteria that are not easily achieved by most gay men.

The idea of having preferences is normal and predictable to a certain extent. However, gay men who maintain rigid expectations for maximum compliance with superficial M-Ranking qualities may wind up with zero returns; they may learn that they can't fulfill a superficial dream of perfection or acquire someone who fits their idealized image. Insisting that gay men achieve systemic compliance with a straight-acting, straight-passing status for oneself and others as part of this collective search is generally a losing battle. They essentially create a situation where nothing is ever good enough.

CHAPTER 8

M-RANKING #2: Manhood—Penis Size, Sexual Appeal, and Performance

Penis size is a symbolic and sensitive issue that also links to a fundamental valuation of masculinity in the GMC.

Meeting expectations for penis size is challenging for gay men because most men are average by definition; much of the GMC's collective preoccupation with penis size persists beyond the capacity of masculinity or sex appeal.

The reality is that the majority of men, whether born gay or straight, have an ordinary, average endowment of about 5 inches erect.[17] Yet gay men are known to perceive a larger endowment to be a highly desirable trait that is more appealing and a sign of greater power.[18] Gay men obsessed with penis size are sometimes referred to as *size queens*. Some gay men place so much value on penis size that they will restrict dating and sexual liaisons with those who are not well-endowed. The size obsession maintains that having sex with a man who has an average or smaller endowment is unfulfilling.

Some gay men are less concerned about penis size. However, it is apparent that portions of the GMC support and promote a collective, socially reinforced norm that considers a well-endowed man to be an enormous turn-on; the hyperfocus of penis size, or manhood, applies initially and primarily to sexual liaisons, but the underlying sentiment is present in many gay connections. The sometimes-unyielding prioritization with having a large endowment can have serious consequences; the implied requirement is one more measurement where gay men can feel deficient, leading to feelings of inadequacy, anxiety, and fear of rejection. Larger-than-average penis size is unobtainable for most gay men, causing more unnecessary feelings of defectiveness to overcome.

"Hung?" High Potential for Hard Blocking if Manhood Size Demands Not Met

Apps and online accounts commonly include the one-word headline of "Hung" in their profile description. Some gay men will lead an inquiry or profile response with the term as a captivating, yet crass, one-word tagline question—"Hung?" or "How big?"—or as a militant, one-line demand for photographic verification. In some instances, if the expected manhood size is not confirmed or is proven to be untrue, the seeker may immediately disengage, including literally blocking any interaction with this person/profile. This cutthroat, indifferent approach is observed as a well-established and socially reinforced norm among some gay men. Clients have reported being rejected in the middle of a liaison that was abruptly ended due to dissatisfaction with endowment size.

Some gay men feel threatened and unsettled about their average-to-small penis size; this is regardless of other M-Ranking criteria or any potential qualities they may possess. Gay men with smaller-than-average penises, particularly a very small or sometimes genetically underdeveloped micropenis, may feel less manly and less confident.

Other than sketchy surgical procedures with marginal outcomes, men are generally unable to change their penis size. Some men who self-identify as average or have a smaller endowment have established healthy self-worth, while others may feel powerless carrying a private, unsettling feeling of being deficient. Coming to a place of self-acceptance of penis size is another area that may require diligent inner work to unravel the heavy influence of the scrutiny of male perfection in the GMC.

Dissatisfaction Caused by Influence of Pornography, Gay Marketing, and Social Media Promotion

Pornography continues to be a massive industry with an enormous following, especially for sexually charged gay men.[19] Gay-centric publications, websites, and apps not only reinforce valuing perfection and model looks, but they also tend to overvalue having a relatively substantial penis size as being sexier and more desirable.

I have heard many single and partnered gay male clients voice concern about their sex lives. They report dissatisfaction with their sexual chemistry and intimacy with their partners, boyfriends, or mates. This is further complicated by comparing themselves, their boyfriends, sex partners, and husbands to the images of actual male models and pornography actors in the adult entertainment industry.

> **CRITICAL THINKING CHOICE CHECKPOINT #9**
>
> What are the actual advantages of being well-endowed? Are gay men who have a larger endowment or who are associated with or dating a more well-equipped man more gratified? Gay men can individually or collectively reconsider how their value system is overly judgmental, limiting, and unnecessarily dismissive in numerous ways. Explore establishing more reasonable expectations for potentially amazing men, most of whom have average equipment, average looks, and average levels of masculine traits.

Some of the male models may be well-endowed; yet they represent a minority of men. One lesson here is about de-emphasizing comparisons, especially the idealization of male sex models and porn actors. These value judgments support a dynamic among gay men that may not change significantly. Those taking issue with penis size must consider personally modifying how they are affected by *all* value judgments; this way they could become more self-accepting by adjusting their own judging.

> **IDEALIZED THOUGHTS ABOUT THE M-RANKING OF "MANHOOD" FOR SOME GAY MEN CAN BE MOTIVATED BY AN ANTI-GAY SUBTEXT**
>
> Some gay men make the following presumptions about the benefits of having or being associated with a larger manhood in the GMC:
>
> » ⊡ I will have a better sex life: more sex, a stronger sex drive, better-quality sex, improved satisfaction, and more validation from sex partners, including more physical fulfillment. ⊡
>
> » ⊡ I will have a greater sense of power, being or feeling more in demand over others, particularly other gay men. ⊡
>
> » ⊡ I will have a more masculine image. ⊡
>
> » ⊡ I will have "bragging rights," amazing, elevated confidence, or a "trophy boyfriend." ⊡
>
> » ⊡ Being more masculine is preferred because it looks less gay. ⊡
>
> » ⊡ Being straight is better and safer than being gay. ⊡
>
> » ⊡ Being gay is bad.

Gay men who struggle with their perception of not being endowed enough and not a good-enough person can modify their thinking; this body part is biologically based and not readily changeable, similar to the way that being born gay is not something that can be changed.

Another thought to consider is the *extent of* energy and focus that gay men contribute to this collective belief. An alternative option is to de-emphasize the impact of what other people, especially gay men, think about you in all capacities, not just endowment. Individual gay men can choose to learn to retreat from self-defining based on external approval, including views about physical attributes. Consider removing yourself from those who continue to judge and dismiss others who don't *measure up.*

CHAPTER 9

M-RANKING #3: Model Looks and Muscles, Youthfulness, and the Power of Visual Perfection

Being fit, healthy, muscular, lean, and in shape has positive and practical benefits. Health benefits include strengthening immune systems and the development of solid muscles supporting a stronger orthopedic system that protects internal organs and multiple bodily functions. A muscular physique can impact and strengthen cardiovascular systems, blood pressure, cholesterol, sugar levels, and body fat. A complete definition of wellness includes the complementary interconnectedness of emotional, social, psychological, and spiritual health. Getting and staying physically fit can be a positive, constructive, fun social activity that doesn't involve drugs or alcohol. It is also a healthy way to stay calm and have a constructive outlet for routine stress and anger management.

In the GMC, there is a heavy emphasis on aesthetics and physical attraction, and a massive focus on sex appeal and sexuality. In addition to being seen as more masculine, being fit and in above-average physical shape does look more attractive to most. Gay men learn that having an above-average physical appearance or being with someone who has an above-average physical appearance is highly valued by many other gay men; this is especially relevant when comparing to other gay men and other people in general who are aesthetically average, not especially fit, or not youthful in appearance. Other perceived benefits include:

- **Opportunity:** Many perceive that being more attractive connotes popularity and will lead to additional opportunities, such as dating, career prospects, and other coveted social associations.
- **Power:** Commanding admiration and positive response from others, especially other gay men, is a show of power.
- **Safety:** An above-average physical appearance shows normalcy, protection, (size) armor, and physical defense.
- **Strength:** Having an aesthetically preferred image and physique may be a show of strength, determination, accomplishment, and also resilience for some.
- **Supremacy:** With an attractive physical appearance comes an opportunity to feel superior, stronger than, bigger than, more attractive than, and better than someone else.
- **Validation:** Having the right image is an opportunity and an outlet for positive feedback, validation, and attention, particularly relevant to gay men who have an extensive history of invalidation.

Muscles, Compensation Efforts, and Narcissism

Being in pristine physical shape is a sought-after health goal. However, gay men may be more preoccupied with obtaining the visually attractive, perfect body. They sometimes transform the pragmatic priorities of achieving a level of health and fitness into an imprudent priority of *looking* healthy and fit with less concern for actually *being* healthy and fit. Becoming captivated by the pursuit of a superior M-Ranking may lead to confusing the intended reasons for exercise and healthiness with seeking aesthetic benefits.

Gay men may be more sexually focused after a history of being or feeling sexually repressed; by prioritizing visual aesthetics, they create a connection to an idealized sense of power and validation. It is as though they hope having model-like looks will generate attention, validation, and sexual fulfillment from other gay men, which it sometimes does. Their motivation is masked by what would otherwise be some textbook health benefits, such as achieving adequate physical exercise and an overall general sense of well-being.

Is Working Out Not Working Out?

"The gym" or similar general descriptions for various health club settings is an important, familiar reference for gay men. Having some type of fitness or gym membership is also presumed to be standard practice for many gay men. Compared to a bar, gyms and fitness centers are places where the social dynamic is predictably healthier and more sober. Some gay men are less aware or don't care that their efforts to be thriving and fit are more a function of being circularly healthy; achieving wellness may be secondary to obtaining sought-after status and sex appeal based on aesthetic accomplishments.

Pairing with or being a man with a model physique is an armor of protection, but it can also be a superficial deflection from resolving more deep-seated internalized inadequacies such as feeling blocked and not man enough or masculine enough. Theoretically, exercise and "working out" include the intention of gaining health, wellness, and stress management benefits. However, health and physical benefits from exercise and alleged wellness goals can be a façade for an underlying superficial intention.

> *Some gay men confuse their intention to achieve a superior state of holistic health and fitness with trying to look more manly and model-like.*

Some gay men confuse their intention to achieve a superior state of holistic health and fitness with trying to look more manly and model-like; some who do look more aesthetically fit also exhibit an inflated sense of supremacy over other gay men. Hence, at various points in the lives of many gay men, *working out is not just working out* when the primary goal is not necessarily about pristine health, fitness, and well-being.

There are certainly benefits to being and looking healthy, fit, and full of sex appeal. However, gay-centric media, advertising, and marketing consistently reflect an enormously high value for a perfected physicality.[20] Online and application (app) profiles commonly reflect gay men boasting about how they love fitness and being active. These values collectively influence the GMC; they may be trying to impress other gay men. Looking "hot," buffed, or striking enough becomes an obsessive priority for many gay men in social and sexual hookups and dating circles. Working out to cultivate a hot, muscled, and theoretically more masculine body is a way to create sexual curb appeal.

Distorted Body Images and Distorted Thinking: A Muscular Physique Equals Masculine Power

The high valuation put on model looks and muscular bodies is common for gay men throughout their adult years. Muscles and classic masculine physical beauty represent a special degree and show of strength, control, and power to gay men.

Both straight and gay men with more serious body image issues (some of which do include actual diagnosed conditions[21] like body dysmorphic disorder [BDD]) commonly have a history of being and feeling belittled and experiencing emotional and physical bullying as a younger boy. This is sometimes relative because they appear less fit, less athletic, or not developed yet compared to their peers.

Gay boys who experience physical deficiencies or obesity while growing up are likely to have greater sensitivity to these issues as adults. Feeling physically compromised, small, weak, fat, or athletically awkward can be damaging to any boy; it impacts gay boys, who are vulnerable to a higher incidence of verbal, physical, and emotional abuse in general, even more. These early experiences are more detrimental to a gay boy who is already progressing from a baseline of internal turmoil and external invalidation. By adulthood, gay men have a higher incidence of body image issues, including BDD; many create a protective armor to achieve a "perfect," attractive, strong, powerful, and muscular body.[22]

"No Fats or Fems": Communal Intolerance of Obesity and Imperfection in the GMC

Despite having subgroups such as bears or chubby chasers, where being overweight or having a larger build is somewhat fetishized, obesity is highly frowned upon collectively in the GMC; it diametrically contradicts the M-Ranking hypervaluation of aesthetic qualities. Those who subscribe to the M-Ranking influence frequently devalue deconditioned, overweight, and even "average" physiques. One association may be that fatness and being overweight suggest unappealing, feminine weakness, which directly defies the prioritization of masculinity and straight-acting and -passing capabilities (regardless of their ostensible level of masculinity).

The GMC is known for being judgmental and critical about fatness, especially overweight gay men.[23] Some gay men (not dissimilar to many Americans, even if they are overweight) are inclined to associate someone who is overweight, out of shape, or obese with unattractiveness, undesirability, inadequacy, weakness, and femininity. Gay male subgroups have emerged, like bears, chubs, and chubby chasers, that normalize or prioritize heavier set, "beefy," and hairy gay men in a more affirmative validating capacity. Gay men supposedly pride themselves on promoting body positivity, diversity,

> *Despite a construct of alleged tolerance, gay men scrutinize matters such as visual appearance, physical challenges, race, and ethnicity.*

inclusiveness, and less superficial judgment. However, this is not always authentically expressed. Despite a construct of alleged tolerance, gay men scrutinize matters such as visual appearance, physical challenges, race, and ethnicity. Being overweight and out of shape is not healthy, but more important (and overemphasized by many gay men) is that *fatness is less attractive*, which is highly deterring to many visually driven gay men.

Most Gay Men Are Not Professional Models

Most people will never look like professional models or movie stars. However, gay men tend to be enthralled by beauty and the quest for a similar caliber of perfection. Attractiveness for some gay men may also require being exceptionally striking in overall appearance. Some will implement unrealistically strict standards and only envision being with another man who satisfies their perception of a perfect, handsome face and physique.

This idealized person would look like a professional model, which sounds phenomenal, except that most men are *not* professional models, including those presumptuous gay men pursuing this level of perfection; that pool is tiny. Gay men who get stuck in this obsession find it difficult to break free and modify their thinking. Inviting them to seek more appropriate, obtainable mates deflates the fantasy. Consequently, maintaining stringent requirements may produce meager returns.

A certain percentage of gay men do have above-average looks, physique, and endowment. Tragically, only some of these men are genuinely confident and truly happy with themselves.

Despite the external presumption that they have it all, many gay men who some would consider physically captivating project an arrogant, feigned confidence to compensate for their underlying insecurity; they self-sabotage the development of constructive, more genuine relationships in the process. This is confirmed by assessing the quantity of single, otherwise eligible/actively dating and attractive, seemingly successful gay men over the age of 45 who remain single.[24]

Over the Gay Hill: The GMC's Obsession with Youthfulness

In addition to the extensive and excessive focus on physical attractiveness, there is also a component of how youthful and fresh one might look. Other than a mostly fetishized "daddy" designation for older and/or more "mature" gay men, many gay men are highly sensitive and commonly judgmental about older ages. The GMC is known to uphold younger men as more desirable; the negative bias forms an undercurrent that seems applicable, even toward gay men, beginning around age 40. Gay men perceive youthfulness as superior, similar to a stereotypical straight male vision of younger women. Gay men are likely to align with superficial values as they associate the concept of youth with a variety of beliefs.

Youthfulness is attractive and desirable, but rigidly *requiring* it, either for self or others, adds to counterproductive, restrictive value judging that results in a lack of successful relationships.

ASSOCIATIONS WITH YOUTHFULNESS

Youth is associated with

» A fresh, new, more attractive appearance

» More (potential) energy physically and sexually

» A better body; "hotter" physique and muscularity

» More attractive face and skin, with less potential for being or looking haggard

» Being perceived as a "better catch" and more acceptable to others, especially in the GMC

Ageism in the GMC: Marginalizing "Older" Gay Men

Younger gay men might throw older gay men an occasional bone of response, attention, or validation. However, for the most part, and beginning for gay men in their 40s, many of them remain romantically unattached. Even if they aren't deliberately taking an active role in seeking perfection, gay men must still contend with the impact of a collective value system perpetuated by other gay men who are more inclined to be seeking perfection; some of this is influenced by the M-Ranking qualities.

Some individual gay men are less beholden to the M-Ranking dynamic; however, much of the "inventory" they draw from in the GMC is highly impacted by the M-Ranking-seeking process and effect. This is not to suggest anyone should quickly and automatically just accept everyone else or disregard personal needs and desires. However, it *is* about establishing constructive, *realistic* priorities and expectations for dating and the appropriateness of another potential gay male partner, date, or mate. This is particularly relevant for older gay men who insist on only dating or mating with much younger gay men who are most often not an appropriate match by multiple measurements.

Even if they aren't deliberately taking an active role in seeking perfection, gay men must still contend with the impact of a collective value system perpetuated by other gay men who are more inclined to be seeking perfection.

Does Life Improve with Age for Gay Men in the GMC?

Aging is a multifaceted process and a sometimes challenging issue for anyone to contend with. For gay men, dealing with the aging process can be even more complicated. The history of being socially delayed and having unresolved issues frequently lingers well past a gay man's 20s, 30s, and beyond; this pattern can include frequent disappointments and losses that feel as though they are built on a compounding history of disillusionment. The more rejections and disappointments experienced along the way, the more some aging gay men become disgusted, frustrated, hopeless, or desperate.

Because the likelihood of past failure and rejection is greater for gay men, and they often continue to experience failure and rejection as they age, they may become pessimistic, overlooking and minimizing the potential for positive growth and improvements moving forward. Thus, for the average gay man who is still struggling with self-acceptance, experiences of failure and rejection may seem exponentially more severe as they age.

Reality for Gay Men Aging into Their 40s and Beyond

Age discrimination in the GMC becomes socially contagious in a sense. A gay male in his 40s, 50s, or older will likely experience, or has already encountered, being or feeling rejected, discarded, and dismissed by some other gay men based solely on their age.

Although being over the age of 40 may not seem that old, some of the GMC, including the 40+ crowd of gay men, have also deemed even their own, more mature age groups to be an "older" crowd. There is a constant flow of younger, newer, and fresher gay men added to the social and dating pool. As they age, even moderately younger gay men can quickly be labeled "older" and, thus, considered less desirable as they eventually compete with younger gay men.

The Vicious Cycle of Youth Obsession in the GMC

Older gay men may still promote a similar value judgment and negative bias about other older gay men.[25] This can include narcissistic rejection by aloof, arrogant gay men who haven't evolved despite their own aging and lack of perfection.

Perhaps most disconcerting of all, some of the gay men who

maintain arrogant aloofness about their contemporaries have little business being so smug. Some older gay men will try to appear young again by seeking plastic surgery or similar services. Others will strive to be associated with a "trophy" companion/boyfriend who is young and full of sex appeal. The result is a tendency for some older gay men to develop an aversion to dating age-appropriate gay men, looking instead for the "ideal," a perfect younger man. Yet, ironically, younger men may be generally disinterested in older gay men because they, too, follow the M-Ranking requirements. And so, a well-engrained cycle of rejection and invalidation is further perpetuated.

As the cycle continues, older and average-looking gay men who are "swimming out of their pool" may be repeatedly judged, rejudged, rejected, or feel socially disposed of and designated as undesirable. Some gay men over 40 struggle to accept the implications of aging, including how other gay men perceive and respond to the aging process. The improved, collective acceptance of aging in the GMC will be slow to change at best.

Remarkably, despite previous experiences and recurrent variations of this same superficial and inappropriate pursuit, the behavior persists. Many of these superficial ageist values are based on a false sense of self and false, less realistic expectations of the M-Ranking influence on a gay man's "market value."

… CHAPTER 10

M-RANKING #4: Money and Material Wealth Can Supplement Other M-Ranking Values

Money and materialism are additional factors of a perceived hierarchy in the GMC. As gay men transition from childhood into gay male adulthood, they come from a variety of financial backgrounds and socioeconomic statuses.

As they acclimate to the GMC dynamics, gay men may come to realize that "money power" is a valuable commodity and a critical element of the M-Ranking equation. They discover that gay men appreciate wealth and nicer material things. Even if they have not yet accumulated wealth, they might attempt to project the image of being wealthy, while some will become motivated by opportunism.

Money and Material Wealth Equal Power to Substitute, Have, or "Buy" the Other Ms

The M-Ranking components are predominantly related to appearance, masculinity, and a straight-acting power position. A substantial value is also placed on having lovely material possessions. Money equals potential power, comfort, and convenience, and it is also a nice accoutrement for the other M-Ranking qualities.

Money power is influential and sometimes used to counterbalance the other M-Ranking values. Having financial means is an advantage and can also be considered an alternate premium value in lieu of possessing the other M-Ranking characteristics.

Money Can't Buy Love, but It's a Starting Point

Financial security may have different significance to gay men than straight men. Typically, gay men in their 40s, 50s, 60s, and beyond have accumulated or have more access to assets and resources. If there is enough money present to take care of another, this can be a powerful appealing option to another gay man who has less security, money, resources, and connections.

> *Money power is influential and sometimes used to counterbalance the other M-Ranking values.*

Greater wealth may lead to connections and networking for employment and other situations influenced by nepotism; this is especially relevant to another in need in competitive, potentially lucrative industries like entertainment, finance, or real estate. A gay man in need may not intentionally think in a calculating manner, but another gay man with significant resources can be financially helpful. As gay men age, some may feel less attractive and also notice the pressure stemming from ageist value judging in the GMC. Financial means or similar resources and connections serve to counterbalance the other aesthetically driven disparities of the M-Ranking variables.

Wealthy men offer several perks, even if they lack other M-Ranking values and aesthetic qualities. Their money and access to a certain type of lifestyle are intriguing and inviting to some gay men, even when there is little or no physical attraction.

Most gay men who live openly gay lives do not have a traditional scenario of a wife and children, and many remain single. Some report receiving punitive restrictions, conditional financial support, removal from potential inheritances, or being cut off from financial support because of their family's threatening intolerance of their gayness.[26] If they are unattached, gay men are less likely to have a comparable level of financial support from a significant other as opposed to straight men who may be married or attached to another income earning spouse.

Most gay men don't have a traditional scenario of a wife and children.

Money Equals More Power, or Filling Voids: The Wealth Continuum in the GMC

Money and similar forms of wealth can create buying power and a sense of supremacy. More purchasing power, plus good fashion, design, material tastes, and awareness of the "gay touch," may offer more opportunities to fill emotional voids with material things.

Those lower on the wealth continuum in the GMC are apt to perceive wealthy gay men as superior, prestigious, and more powerful. In my practice, I have observed that the less wealthy, less financially successful gay men sometimes allow themselves to feel subjugated and become envious of wealthier gay men; this may also include a sense of resentment of other people who are perceived to be more successful, wealthier, and more powerful in general.

CHAPTER 11

M-RANKING #5: Mainstream Compatibility in Both Straight and Gay Environments

For the purposes of this discussion, the concept of the mainstream heterosexual world consists of men and women who are predominantly heterosexual, referring to individuals who were assigned male or female at birth and who identify with their assigned gender. Today, mainstream heterosexuals are sometimes referred to as cis male and cis female, and they comprise the majority of people.

The healthier side of a mainstream version in the GMC offers a sense of community and support. The GMC can provide an affirming framework where gay men can connect with other men in a variety of ways. Unfortunately, some of the mainstream norms in the GMC present mixed aspects, including periodic doses of ultra-conformity and rejection. Less desirable qualities are associated with what should be a sense of support and community.

Blending In with Both Straight and Gay Worlds

Mainstream appeal outside the GMC becomes relevant as an ability to join and pass as heterosexual or somehow be more accepted in the straight world. Some gay men are more capable of, more aware of, more willing to, and more interested in actively trying to blend into the mainstream straight world, which can be an advantage. The capacity to more easily conform to desirable, mainstream society may result in a higher ranking and more normalized image for gay men within the collective aspects of the GMC. If a gay man has high compliance with other M-Ranking variables, he presumes he will be more confident and will likely possess more solid levels of mainstream appeal in both straight and gay circles. This drive to seek social approval and acceptance sounds and feels similar to adolescent stage social climbing.

Mainstream Appeal and Avoiding Mediocrity

The M-Ranking pursuit of mainstream elements is influenced by earlier learned hetero-preferred values. This holdover comes with a limiting set of more superficial values, like being straight-acting. These values are related to a long-engrained history that appears more affirming in regard to straightness.

A more mature, evolved, enlightened gay man will see beyond this simplicity and learn they may have idealized mainstream acceptance; they will also see more clearly that the mainstream version of conformity in the GMC is equally limiting. Unfortunately, some gay men minimize the consequences of a blocked, non-gay-affirmative viewpoint.

If gay men choose to continue to overvalue these traits they learned from their childhood years as gay boys, they limit their growth and ability to facilitate authentic intimacy.

High School Is Over; Gay Men Now Seek an Ideal Gay Prototype

The thought of being "just average" can be highly undesirable to some gay men. Gay men may have a need to overachieve and be the best—or at least better than the next. High school and adolescent stages, which some adult gay men seem to be stuck at, are a time when prioritizing mainstream conformity is more predictable and customary; this mentality

> *Gay men may have a need to overachieve and be the best—or at least better than the next.*

supports a desperate effort to fit in and obey some perceived norm. Some gay men struggle to move beyond high school social climbing, where there is a comparable emulation to conform to masculine norms.[27]

The propensity for default conformity is an unpleasant memory for gay boys who may have blindly followed the influences of a devaluing, straight-dominated, straight-normalized childhood environment.

> ### CRITICAL THINKING CHOICE CHECKPOINT #10
> The pursuit of the perfect M-Ranking in the GMC is somewhat contradictory. One goal is to begin to unblock by releasing the perceived destructive pressure of conforming to stereotypically straight-normal social norms. However, gay men may be faced with an ironic need to conform again *within* the GMC; for some, this consists of a paradox of even more pressure to be straight-acting or perceived as perfect by adhering to the M-Ranking qualities, which are difficult to achieve or obtain.

Gay men have to work through lingering emotional fatigue to let go of residual pressure to conform as they come out and into some aspect of the GMC; they need to de-emphasize any new variation of pressure to conform (i.e., the M-Ranking) while living as an openly gay man in the GMC.

Gay men must accept that it is unlikely that they will become or obtain the idealized image of a model or porn star; they can elect to own and acknowledge their gayness by maximizing the simplicity of just being themselves.

Gay men must accept it is unlikely that they will become or obtain the idealized image of a model or porn star.

Regardless, some gay men will still feel pressured to conform to mainstream ideals. Some of the mainstream conformity and stringent, exceptional standards within the GMC contribute to a value system that includes an official determination of what is good and bad; even worse, parts of the GMC dynamics may collectively operate to determine *who* is good and *who* is bad.

The grasp of the M-Ranking-seeking mainstream dynamics in the GMC can be powerful and extensive. Gay men can resist mainstream conformity efforts. Even with individual high self-esteem levels and recovery, the ability to deflect the element of conformity-based mainstream gay ideals (i.e., avoiding social climbing similar to high school cliques) is still challenging.

PART III

Ramifications of Straight Male Privilege on Gay Men

CHAPTER 12

Straight Male Privilege: A Different Life of Unforeseen Advantages for Heterosexual Men

The concept of *privilege* has gained attention recently in discussions about political climates or more specifically related to identity politics. Privilege, in this sense, refers to unearned or unfair advantages that are not warranted due to systemic inequities, particularly racial differences, and in that capacity, it is frequently associated with the term *White privilege*. For example, White privilege implies that White/Caucasian/noncolored people enjoy advantages in society not afforded to people of color, particularly Black Americans. In this definition, the absence of privilege typically leads to facing disadvantages and challenges. These difficulties may include social, political, and financial outcomes.

The reality of privilege and its impact in the United States has an extensive history, especially prior to the civil rights movement of the 1960s, which led to the Civil Rights Act of 1964. This was accomplished after extensive political and social advocacy for legal equality and rights for minorities. The US Civil Rights Act was especially relevant to Black Americans, who had been openly discriminated against in many social, legal, and political capacities. Gay (LGBT) legal rights weren't as substantially addressed until 2015, more than 50 years later, when gay people gained the equal right to marry, be openly gay in the military, and thereafter, to be included in an officially sanctioned list that offers stipulations for legal protection from being discriminated against based on sexual orientation.[28]

Different Perceptions of Privilege

In recent years, the reference to privilege, when discussed in the context of societal hierarchies, has become controversial and elicits a wide range of emotionally charged reactions. The privilege implications are based, to some degree, on value judgments and perceptions and predominantly refer to the birthright of those considered to be privileged (as opposed to a more specific, narrow definition of privilege, such as explicitly having more wealth and resources or what some generally refer to as a "privileged childhood"). When speaking of straight male privilege or White privilege, this typically covers different measurable characteristics not directly related to money, such as sexual or racial identity or racial appearance. In this sense, the existence, presence, and perception of privilege are often based on long-standing, collectively driven societal norms that have also been historically reinforced both legally and politically.

A portion of people from a multitude of races, ethnicities, and cultures believe that certain minority groups (generally non-White) have multiple difficulties and unfair challenges because of not having the same options that others (predominantly White people) have, hence the term *White privilege*. Those who promote and support the implication of the term and concept of *privilege* argue that it is highly relevant to social norms and social status. Privilege is a consequence of and results in various biases, but it is often misunderstood, too; it is therefore automatically but potentially incorrectly associated with racism and other forms of discrimination, like anti-gay/LGBTQ. For example, some will argue that those who have been historically marginalized, like Black or gay people, are *always* subjected to the inequity and inadequacies of *not* having privilege; this overgeneralization automatically renders these groups as victims because it presumes *all* of them automatically feel and have a sense of deficiency compared to White or straight people.

Some Deny That Privilege Exists

Also critical to note is that those who deny the existence, presence, and influence of privilege, including social privilege, contend that privilege, particularly White privilege, does not exist or, at a minimum, does not exist anymore. They insist that alleging someone has more privilege over others is a baseless, self-righteous excuse for one's failures or inadequacies. Those who don't believe in the existence and impact of privilege will argue that there is legal and political *equality,* so there can't really be any remnant or impact of privilege.

I contend that privilege, including straight privilege, should not be used as an excuse, *but that doesn't deny the history and present existence and impact of privilege in this sense.*

The Reality of Privilege

There has been impressive progress toward improved legal and political equality. However, the *social stigma* influence doesn't necessarily diminish. Despite the idea that some consider legal equality a sufficient extinguishment of the presence and impact of privilege, various forms of privilege linger in a mixed, diverse society. **The reality is that most gay men do not have straight privilege because they are not straight.** I am not labeling gay men as victims either, but being aware of the implications of straight male privilege is important.

Straight Male Privilege Offers Covert and Overt Advantages to Straight Men

Straight male privilege is the notion that heterosexual males enjoy a range of explicit or less obvious benefits and advantages when compared to those of gay males. Most men are heterosexual, which makes belonging to this vast majority already a privilege in some regard. Straight male privilege is a critical concept to comprehend; it is much more than trendy, politically correct rhetoric. Privilege, in reference to gay men and blocking, is determined by examining the different experiences and opportunities that straight men have compared to gay men.

> **CRITICAL THINKING CHOICE CHECKPOINT #11**
>
> **The purpose of discussing and understanding the relativity of straight male privilege is** to create awareness that it is harder being a gay man. It is beneficial to anyone who cares about gay men and gay men themselves to affirm that straight male privilege exists. Acknowledging privilege means understanding that gay men are prone to both overt and less obvious disadvantages of being automatically judged, criticized, and penalized in various capacities solely because they are gay men.
>
> My reason for discussing privilege in *You've Been Blocked* is not to make straight men or anyone else feel bad, nor is it for gay men to be portrayed as victims, nor is it because these comments will change the phenomenon of privilege. It is being discussed to validate gay men and increase understanding about the lives of gay men. The impact of straight male privilege is relevant to gay men; it is real and is not going away.

My intention is to refer to straight male privilege as a well-established process that will almost certainly remain as a social construct. Long-standing values and beliefs hold that heterosexuality is more common and deemed more traditionally normal by the mainstream world compared to homosexuality.

Gay men are a vast minority, and being gay comes with certain disadvantages. Gay men were subjected to more legal and political inequality in past generations through unfair laws, restrictions, and more openly systemic anti-gayness. Acknowledging the existence of straight male privilege can induce uncomfortable reactions from some straight people. Some of them can acknowledge the presence of privilege, while others do not see it, don't believe it, or don't care, while others deny or minimize its implications.

Straight male privilege occurs in a dynamic similar to the way the sometimes subtle yet penetrating privilege or differences in experience, various opportunities, and societal reactions manifest between Black and White people. While the story is not always the same, gay men are more likely to have had a difficult childhood, which can influence the next stages of their lives.

There are many negative views still maintained about gay men. Straight men will not be scrutinized in a comparable manner; they are less likely to be shamed, invalidated, harassed, disrespected, and blocked *at a basic level because* of their heterosexual ("straight-normal") orientation.

CRITICAL THINKING CHOICE CHECKPOINT #12

Certain aspects of straight male privilege have been significantly reduced or eliminated after improved legal and political regulation of equal rights for gay people were created and implemented. However, less obvious implications of (mostly) *social* straight male privilege will likely persist.

Straight Male Privilege Creates a Profoundly Different Reality for Gay Men from Childhood to Adulthood

The various forms of straight male privilege contain several important distinctions. Initially, adult gay males do not have the "right" or the opportunity of having a history of a straight male childhood "behind them." This means gay boys face numerous challenges that can negatively impact their adult lives early on compared to their straight peers.

The effects of privilege remain, whether they are overtly obvious and relevant or not. Every person has the option to decide whether they want to accept that various forms of privilege exist. Some gay men have chosen to accept the reality that straight male privilege exists and have learned to work around it. In general, denying that straight men at least have some unacknowledged advantages compared to gay men is not accurate and not particularly validating.

Gay men should be mindful that choosing to blame or rationalize various personal life challenges that arise due to straight male privilege may create self-imposed victimization. Blaming one's adversity on not having privilege is unproductive and can be displaced, creating additional hateful resentment towards others who are viewed to have more power; individuals impacted by disparities must rise above the external impact of privilege. Inequity, as opposed to inequality, is not a constructive excuse for one's struggles, despite how unfair, frustrating, and challenging those obstacles may be or feel.

Examples of the Lack of Straight Male Privilege for Gay Men

Straight male privilege takes many forms. Straight males may face adversity or lack some privilege in their lives in other ways, but many of their gay counterparts are affected by a different, more abusive history of being judged or heavily disliked just for being born gay.

Less need to deflect negative judgments and bias. A straight male does not worry about being judged for being gay; he will not be even remotely viewed in the same negative manner for being heterosexual in the first place. A straight male will not have to reinvent himself, thus expending excess energy and angst over what others think of him based on his fundamental sexual identity.

Less concern about family or societal rejection. The average straight man has considerably less worry about his family disowning him, being fired from a job, or being ridiculed, shamed, and degraded because of his sexuality or for having less traditionally masculine behaviors, features, and inflection. A gay male is more likely to have to worry or wonder about how others perceive him in many routine, daily social/vocational/life situations and interactions. A straight male is much less likely to analyze an interaction and wonder, "What do they think of me (and my gayness)?" The greater potential for this type of scrutiny and neurotic worry does not occur for straight men in the same way as it does for many gay men.

A default and fundamental right to be themselves. Straight men automatically have a basic right and option to be themselves comfortably; straight men feel less need to *block*, repress, hide out, and "invisibilize" themselves for fear of unknown punitive consequences for their sexuality. Straight men do not need to be or think "on guard" the way gay men do.

Little or no need to hide or repress. A straight man will not feel comparable pressure to deliberately misrepresent himself as something he is not to accommodate someone or something else. If a straight male is with a female girlfriend, date, partner, or significant other, it is generally presumed that they are romantically or sexually involved; straight men do not feel a need to date women to act as a "beard" to cover up their gayness and keep themselves safe from being judged or perceived negatively for being gay and what some view as abnormal. (Some gay men still choose to cover up their homosexuality by trying to look straight and be with or marry a female.)

Higher default levels of acceptance and self-acceptance. Straight men don't need to "come out" of anywhere. A straight male does not have to confront sexual identity issues as a gay man does; straight men will not have to struggle to learn or relearn self-acceptance. In marked contrast, achieving self-acceptance is sometimes a lifetime burden for a gay man.

A straight man will not have to work as diligently to establish basic self-respect, self-confidence, and self-efficacy in the same way as a gay man does.

More "normal" efforts to get needs met. A straight man generally gets his needs met more readily; he can accomplish this without premeditated planning and prodding, with less disappointment, confusion, and rejection. In contrast, most gay boys grow up learning how to block, hide, and rebrand themselves; they may feel that many of their needs were essentially superficial since their true selves are generally not revealed in the first place.

Routine predictability with clearer boundaries about intimacy. A straight man has abundant opportunity to express himself romantically and sexually through his natural attraction to females, beginning in childhood and adolescence; gay boys and gay men do not. A straight man is more likely to feel comfortable expressing who he is *and* have that persona validated as normal by default in most environments. A straight man may not even realize he is being affirmed, in a sense, just for being normal; gay men are more prone to feel the need to sneak around, wondering who else might be gay and not feeling consistently emotionally safe.

Fewer incidences of routine hatred, bias, discrimination, and abuse. A straight man is less likely to be verbally or physically assaulted for his sexual orientation or anything related to it. Straight men are not betrayed repeatedly when or if they are "found out," nor do they need to strategize a response. Straight men will not be ridiculed, mocked, and verbally accosted with a myriad of anti-gay, derogatory terms like *fag, faggot, queer, bitch,* or *homo.* If a straight man is called a faggot, it's likely one of his straight buddies joking around with him, and it means something entirely different; the comparable use of anti-gay slurs among and between straight men are generally *not* driven by egregious hate or reckless, dismissive ignorance.

Different relationship with HIV and AIDS. Potentially, anyone who is sexually active can be exposed to or contract a sexually transmitted disease, including human immunodeficiency virus (HIV). However, HIV and AIDS (acquired immunodeficiency syndrome) bring both historical and current contexts that are more relevant to gay men and the GMC. A straight man is less likely to wonder and worry about being exposed to HIV or *seroconversion* (becoming HIV-positive) after sexual encounters with women; straight men are less likely to be hyperaware and mindful about HIV affecting them because it doesn't affect them in that capacity.

Many gay men are still more knowledgeable about and impacted by HIV transmission than straight men are. A straight man (mostly those born prior to 1980) probably did not have numerous friends and acquaintances die of AIDS; many gay men did experience unthinkable loss, sometimes at catastrophic levels, particularly between the 1980s and the mid-1990s. A straight male does not encounter the collective trauma and emotional injuries produced for decades by the AIDS epidemic and the related fight for gay rights.

> **CRITICAL THINKING CHOICE CHECKPOINT #13**
>
> Straight male privilege has lessened somewhat, but it is still here and is not going away. The impact of straight male privilege will remain present, even when engaging with more tolerant, aware, informed, progressive, and less judgmental heterosexual men and women. Straight male privilege will remain even if straight or gay people are not fully aware of its presence or if a gay man does not feel as personally impacted as another gay man may feel. *It is happening somewhere around you.* Gay men know this because they live this.

Basic "Life Rights." Gay men still lack certain basic "life rights," including a comparable option to flirt and engage freely with the same sex. At a fundamental level of human behavior and social interaction, gay men do not have the same consistent opportunity to express themselves *comfortably* and safely toward members of the same sex in a comparable manner to the way straight men can with members of the opposite sex. This makes gay men more vulnerable to worry. Gay men are more likely to have fears and anxiety about how others perceive them; some will persistently wonder if they are being judged or somehow penalized for being gay or for any other questionable related negative bias because they are different. Lacking clarity and fewer clear boundaries may lead to unpleasant consequences. Gay men are more apt to obsess or worry about being judged, which may also include possibly dangerous, punitive penalties or consequences for seemingly routine or potential engagements with the same sex. When flirting with or propositioning another man or sometimes relative to even less intimate interactions with anyone, gay men have additional matters to consider: they have to wonder if the other person knows they are gay and is even possibly interested, if applicable, if that person is actually gay, and how that person perceives gay men.

> **CRITICAL THINKING CHOICE CHECKPOINT #14**
>
> We live in a predominantly straight world, which is the way things are and which is not bad per se. Being aware of the realities of living in a straight-dominated society doesn't necessarily make it any easier, more pleasant, or less damaging for gay men. This awareness is another reality check that requires gay men to concede that they exist in a straight-dominated society that may require navigation and creative adaptation to accept that the influence of straight male privilege is still present and may always be.

Many gay men feel a sense of unfulfilled yearning. Fantasies are more remote and avoidant and create higher stakes for gay teens and young gay men; some feel anxious when thinking about responding to the object of their same-sex interest. Gay men commonly miss opportunities to comfortably and affirmatively yearn and fantasize about something they should have comparable access to and options for. Gay men may be fearful of the potential consequences of indications of their interest in another man; in addition, they may contend with game playing and rejection when engaging with closeted gay men.

Straight-Acting and Straight-Passing Gay Male Privilege: Actual and Perceived Advantages of "Passing" for Straight

Straight-acting gay male privilege is another variation of straight privilege. The more naturally straight-acting and straight-passing gay men appear and present, the more likely their straight-acting privilege will allow for at least some of the benefits enjoyed by heterosexual men. The true advantage of passing for straight is complicated and debatable. Gay men who visually appear, act, and sound more stereotypically heterosexual are considered by some to have straight-passing, gay male privilege. Gay men with naturally occurring straight-acting privilege are more inclined to pass as heterosexual without becoming overly affected, enacting forced restriction of their gayness, or trying to act tough or hypermasculine.

Straight-passing privilege refers to gay men who are more able to pass for heterosexual, whether they do so naturally or are trying to, and whether they are confident and conscious about their ability to do so or not. Frequently, the more effeminate or less stereotypically straight-appearing boys and teens have a higher incidence of being harassed and bullied;[29] thus, they have less opportunity to be accepted, even superficially, for who and what they are during the critical stages of child and adolescent development.

Blending into the straight-world majority can superficially and temporarily protect straight-passing gay men from what could otherwise be negative treatment if they were more obviously gay (and until they conceivably come out and more openly identify as gay).

Some gay men have a theoretical advantage from passing for straight and are also deliberately trying to keep their gayness hidden or quiet; they can make good use of their ability to pass for straight. Other gay men may possess physical and psychosocial characteristics that are less traditionally, less obviously "gay" but will not attempt to deny or hide their homosexuality.

A Have/Have-Not Disparity Among Gay Men

Gay and straight men appear to respond more positively to more masculine gay men.[30] Straight-acting, or presenting as more masculine, is part of the higher composite value of the M-Ranking scale and creates a disparity. The have/have-not disparity is highly impacted by the ability to pass for straight/heterosexual. Some gay men who are more obviously gay or less stereotypically masculine may feel like a "have-not" because they are prone to harbor resentment toward other more seemingly masculine gay men they perceive to *have* the blessed gift of straight-acting/passing privilege.

In most cases, gay men who are straight-acting and straight-passing will eventually acknowledge their gayness; the truth is usually found out somehow anyway. A gay man who can more easily pass for straight is still a gay man, whether his sexual orientation is more obvious or confirmed or not.

Straight-acting/straight-passing gay male privilege means some gay men have less surface need to block thanks to less obvious gay traits and judgments. Gay boys who are less effeminate and not as obviously gay usually have fewer bullying experiences. In non-gay-affirming environments, such as school settings, they are less prone to overtly degrading treatment.[31] Even if a gay male teen with straight-acting privilege is out or openly gay, he is less likely to be impacted to the same extent that a more effeminate gay boy or teen will be.

Boys who are more effeminate and more identifiably gay might still try to downplay their gay sexual orientation. The majority of gay men with straight-acting privilege will take the opportunity to hide out at some point. The straight-acting gay boy or teen has a different experience. His regular day-to-day activities and interactions are likely somewhat different from those of other gay boys who are unable, less able, or unwilling to repress themselves and their gayness.[32]

Straight-acting gay men may still be distressed about their

sexuality as much as those who are gay-exemplified.[33] However, the gay boy who appears more conventionally masculine is more likely to enter gay male adulthood in both gay and straight worlds with a stronger, less superficially affected or damaged sense of self. When gay sexual orientation is not immediately obvious, it allows some gay men to temporarily lessen the impact of anti-gay discrimination.

Some current social and political movements may presume that straight male privilege is gone or never really existed, *but it does exist* and will not be going away. Those maintaining some anti-gay rationale either don't care about straight male privilege, deny that it exists, or may genuinely believe that straight people *should* have privilege because they are straight.

CRITICAL THINKING CHOICE CHECKPOINT #15

Anyone of any gender or sexual orientation can benefit from learning what straight male privilege is. The effects of straight male privilege will likely always be present in a well-established dynamic that has unanticipated benefits for many heterosexual men.

Three critical points to know:

1. **Straight male privilege is real, continues to exist, and often has a powerful impact on gay men.** It poses a disadvantage for gay men, even if straight people and some gay men are unaware or vehemently deny it exists. Suggesting it hasn't and doesn't pose challenges for gay men is a fallacy.

2. **Social aspects of straight male privilege may not significantly subside or change,** even considering improved legal and political equality for gay men.

3. **Similar to other forms of privilege, straight male privilege is not a viable excuse for problems,** feeling like a failure, succumbing to failure, underachieving, or choosing to remain a victim full of jealousy and resentment of other successful, prolific people.

Gay men can empower themselves by understanding the existence and potential impact of straight male privilege and straight-passing privilege; they should accept that they will likely encounter the impact of straight male privilege because they are gay men. Being aware of the reality of privilege is valuable, but feeling like a disempowered victim is not. Creating or blaming a sense of failure or stagnation on straight male privilege is irresponsible and limiting. Self-evolution will happen through being committed to goals and aspirations despite any encountered or perceived adversity.

CHAPTER 13

I'm Almost Positive: The Striking Impact of HIV/AIDS

I'm almost positive describes the systemic anticipatory anxiety and fear related to the human immunodeficiency virus (HIV) and HIV status felt by many gay men, which was especially elevated during various junctures of the acquired immunodeficiency syndrome (AIDS) epidemic from 1981 to 1996. The impact of HIV and AIDS on the gay male community generated mixed results. A sense of community was strengthened by additional attention and support. However, the fear of potentially contracting HIV and AIDS also triggered a wave of panic, disparity, and criticism that perpetuated value judging between gay men.

Whether gay men were HIV-positive or not, they were almost positive.

After an abrupt onset of AIDS in 1981, HIV was identified as the cause. HIV and AIDS became a widespread epidemic that was particularly catastrophic for gay men. This period brought intense emotional and physical reactions, pain, and suffering; many gay men felt severe fear, anxiety, shame, confusion, anger, and powerlessness. It created rampant, heartbreaking loss and induced a lingering traumatic hypervigilance of persistent fear.

Living in Constant Fear: "Will I Be Next?"

HIV is transmitted mainly through bodily fluids and unprotected as well as promiscuous sexual activity. Men having sex with other men was considered a major risk factor, particularly early on, as the AIDS crisis continued to escalate through the 1980s and early 1990s. Life for many gay men in the GMC after 1981 became fraught with anxiety because of the fears of contracting, suffering, and dying from HIV and AIDS.

In 1981, many considered HIV and AIDS to be a terrifying plague. Although the initial onset was obscure, increasing numbers of gay men became HIV-positive or had acquaintances or significant others in the GMC who became afflicted and, often, terminally ill. Particularly during the earlier years of the 1981 through 1996 AIDS epidemic period, many gay men in the GMC learned of the high risk and soon knew of someone who was critically ill or dying.

AIDS patients were stigmatized in and out of the GMC. At that time, many succumbed to a painful, sometimes isolated, shameful, and frightening death. Testing for HIV was not standardized and approved by the FDA until 1985.

At the onset of AIDS, some gay men struggled to accept the reality and potential severity of becoming HIV-positive. Gay men, who were accustomed to feeling more carefree about casual, frequent sex eventually grew more fearful about sexual activity; they sometimes felt a sense of bargaining, wondering whether they were going to *seroconvert*, which means to become HIV-positive through "transitioning from the point of viral infection to when antibodies of the virus become present in the blood."[34]

Some other gay men who were already diagnosed as HIV-positive felt severe anxiety about if or when they would be diagnosed with AIDS, how their disease would progress, and whether they would even survive. Tragically, after social stigmatization, battling severe physical symptoms, and often being subjected to ineffective medical treatments with disastrous side effects, many died of AIDS anyway. Newer, more effective variations of drugs to treat HIV infection were more widely released in early 1996. Prior to that time, treatment for HIV and AIDS had marginal efficacy.

HIV and AIDS had a critical impact on gay men, the gay rights movement, and the GMC specifically. After AIDS activists spent years of diligent campaigning, advocating, and marching in the streets, politicians and the general public eventually became more aware and responsive to the AIDS crisis and how it was specifically impacting gay men.[35] Ignorant, insensitive people continued to stigmatize and dehumanize gay men as immoral deviants; gay men were sometimes confronted with nasty generalizing slurs, such as "having AIDS," or outrageous attacks suggesting that AIDS was "God's punishment" for being gay. However, a positive shift also happened in other parts of society as they responded with more sensitive, empathetic notice of gay men and gay issues. Eventually, AIDS Project organizations and charities emerged in most major U.S. cities to support those impacted medically, emotionally, and socially.

Younger Gay Men Born After 1980 Are Often Less Aware About AIDS

Younger gay men (born after 1980 or so) generally have been less affected by HIV/AIDS, or if they were, it was in a different capacity than for gay men in earlier generations. Gay men who are just entering the GMC today may have even less awareness of the historical implications of HIV and AIDS.[36]

Younger adult gay men are less likely to relate to the history and the more severe trauma of the epidemic. Regardless, HIV status still factors into the dynamics of how a variety of different ages and generations of gay men judge one another. HIV still exists primarily as a sexually transmitted virus, even if treatment and prevention options have greatly improved. Since the late '90s, there has been a gradual improvement in awareness about this condition and more tolerance in and out of the GMC for those who are HIV-positive.

Detailed education about HIV and AIDS is not the purpose for including this topic. *You've Been Blocked* focuses on a corresponding hierarchy within the GMC but does not address additional, broad, multifaceted details about HIV and AIDS. Part of the dynamics in the GMC include a division between those who feel like haves or have-nots in various capacities; the "have/have-not" influence creates value judgments about HIV status.

HIV-Positive Stigma Is More Relative to Gay Men Than Straight Men

HIV is a virus that can potentially infect anyone regardless of their sexual orientation. However, heterosexual men have not had to deal with HIV in the same capacity as gay men. After more than four decades, HIV is still a relevant issue for gay men. HIV-related issues and the HIV status of individuals have become an integral part of the GMC because they have been closely scrutinized for years.

Gay men are already distressingly familiar with feeling shame and being judged by society and by other gay men. There is less fear and judgment about HIV in the GMC due to evolving awareness, attitudes, treatment, and medical approaches, but it is still present.

Historically, being HIV-positive frequently became an encumbrance for gay men when considering another gay man's viability for dating, sexual liaisons, or similar connections. Even today, with vastly improved medical treatments, reduced transmission, and prophylactic prevention, HIV positivity is still a factor when gay men judge one another.[37] HIV status created unfair variables for gay men, especially in the first half of the more than 40 years that HIV has been a part of the medical/psychosocial framework. The disparity may be even more relative to millions of gay men who were sexually active adults during the 1980s and 1990s; they were subjected to more aggressive, overt discrimination. Even asymptomatic, HIV-positive men sometimes carried a stigma and sense of shame in a similar way to how some of them may have endured their "dirty secret" about being gay. There were situations where gay men had been closeted or discreet but were forcibly "outed" after they or their gay male partner was diagnosed with or died of AIDS. Some of them had little or no family support; others were shunned or rejected by their families or in-laws because of the shame surrounding the entire issue of gayness and the association of HIV and AIDS.[38]

> ### THE INEQUITABLE IMPACT OF THE AIDS EPIDEMIC ON GAY MEN
>
> » Some gay men who were exposed to HIV contracted the virus, becoming HIV-positive, while others who were also exposed, even repeatedly, did not contract the virus, remaining HIV-negative.
>
> » Some HIV-positive men exhibited symptoms; some did not.
>
> » Some required immediate treatment; some did not.
>
> » Some who had the virus died immediately, and some held on longer but later died anyway. Some survivors have been HIV-positive since the early 1980s and are alive today, more than 40 years later.
>
> » Some accessed the drugs and were compliant; some did not access the current treatments or were less compliant with treatment.
>
> » Some responded to treatment well; some did not.
>
> » Some had limited access to early treatment, such as azidothymidine (AZT). AZT was one of the earlier variations of today's widely used HIV treatments consisting of antiretroviral protease inhibitors. The newer derivatives are safer and more effective, and are now used to maintain an "undetectable" (essentially keeping the virus dormant) status in HIV-positive men.
>
> » Some had unprotected sex but did not contract the virus; many having unprotected sex did contract the virus.
>
> » Some contracted the virus after one sexual encounter; others may have had multiple partners before seroconverting, or they did not seroconvert at all.

> » Some became physically and medically impacted and compromised, including physical deformities from the side effects of the medications or the disease itself or both; some did not.
>
> » Some remained negative even before the much later (2012) advent and option of pre-exposure prophylaxis (PrEP), which HIV-negative gay men take to prevent seroconversion to HIV if exposed.
>
> » Some lost unfathomable numbers of friends; some lost fewer or none.
>
> » Some had affirming family/community support; many did not, especially early on.
>
> » Some who thought they were having "safe sex" or were active only in "safer situations" were eventually either betrayed or seroconverted to being positive anyway.

Many Gay Men Were Fearful and Anxious, Sometimes Scared to Death, and Scared *of* Death

The GMC was collectively burdened with worry. HIV-positive men had to be incessantly attentive to their health and treatment modalities; this created additional anxiety about containing the development and progression of AIDS or potentially dying from it. HIV-negative men would worry about contracting HIV and becoming positive. Particularly during and even somewhat after the AIDS epidemic period of 1981–1996, a sense of panic and fear about HIV and fretful attempts to remain HIV-negative and alive exacerbated the have/have-not dynamic. This constant, looming fear of seroconverting to HIV-positive and being stigmatized became a perilous gamble for some. As familiar or empathetic as some gay men may have felt for those living with HIV, being HIV-positive prior to the release of improved treatments in 1996 was especially alarming and ominous to some gay men.

Some HIV-negative gay men maintained adverse value judgments about HIV positivity, perhaps out of self-protection, anxiety, or ignorance. Some gay men developed HIV-phobias and clinical anxiety or panic in response to even trivial and predictable medical symptoms from a cold, flu, sore throat, a spot or mark, or other physical symptoms, and would rush to "get tested." Extensive information, marketing brochures, and "safe sex" guidelines were available in public buildings and agencies, such as STD clinics or the Gay and Lesbian Centers of major cities. These advisements were later renamed saf*er* sex guidelines.

Even when instant oral test results debuted in the late 1990s, some gay men continued to engage in a cycle of:

» Having sex

» Getting tested

» Waiting for results

» Hoping the results were negative and accurate (juggling around the alleged exposure/incubation window estimates)

» Getting tested again to be sure, and then feeling a temporary sense of safety before

» Starting the cycle again after the next potential exposure/sexual liaison

This felt like a nerve-racking gamble with mortality to some and, depending on the results, could add another layer to the value and focus on feeling ashamed and inadequate.

The neurotic, self-imposed gambling-worry cycle would start all over again after obtaining a negative test result. Some gay men insensitively referred to HIV-negative status as being "clean" (versus being "dirty" or HIV-positive); this reference still occurs in the GMC today. Some gay men would have additional, even routine, sex partners with unverifiable levels of compliance with the safer sex guidelines, and then nervously get tested for HIV repeatedly. Even following the safer sex guidelines, particularly using condoms for anal sex, some sexually active gay men suffered from a looming vision of life-threatening scenarios.

Stigma Continues to Surround HIV Status

HIV status still factors into part of the have/have-not disparity and pecking order in the GMC today. Some of the general mainstream population maintain negative impressions about gay men and HIV, despite more than 40 years of progress, education, and awareness. Although making an automatic connection between being a gay man with having AIDS and dying from it was more common in the past, parts of straight mainstream society still judge, criticize, and reject HIV-positive gay men.[39] Some HIV-positive gay men report feeling damaged. Some ignorant people still apparently automatically associate gay men with AIDS.

Younger gay men may appear less concerned about HIV; many are misinformed about HIV and AIDS and not extensively or immediately interested, concerned, or impacted because of their younger ages and presumed lack of relevancy. Yet their ignorance or lack of interest is a problem: The Centers for Disease Control report that gay men ages 25–34 make up the majority of newly diagnosed HIV cases.[40] The generational impact of HIV awareness and judgment contributes to further division in the GMC.

Newer Medical Developments Created "Undetectable" Status for HIV-Positive Men

By the late 1990s, the prognosis for HIV-positive individuals had greatly improved; medical and social models were shifting to treating HIV as a manageable condition rather than a terminal disease. Newer medications and derivatives of previous treatments became more effective at minimizing HIV viral loads; while they did not cure or eliminate the virus, the newer medications after the millennium were often functional enough to create what became known as "undetectable" status. *Poz Magazine* was launched in 1994; it included a newer, abbreviated modification of the term *HIV-positive*.[41] This may have influenced the promotion of a new social term for living with HIV: *healthy poz* as an affirmative reference for living in a healthy capacity with HIV positivity that eventually became known simply as "undetectable."

Medical treatments for HIV have radically improved, with fewer severe side effects. The current treatment options have much less or no side effects and generally involve one pill per day to keep the virus dormant. Most HIV treatments today keep viral loads at minimal levels, which maintains a relatively normal state of health. Consequently, most HIV-positive people receiving these treatments have minimal traces of HIV in their system and are considered "undetectable."

PrEP Medication Approach Introduced

In 2012, the Food and Drug Administration (FDA) approved the use of the drug Truvada as a pre-exposure prophylaxis, known as PrEP. This approach involved using the same or similar medications that are utilized for treating those already diagnosed with HIV (HIV-positive). The goal of prescribing PrEP was to prevent seroconversion in HIV-negative people in case there was HIV exposure.[42] Using PrEP to prevent HIV contraction is reported to be as effective as 99% with adequate drug levels (and compliance as per physician care and treatment plan.)[43] The option of PrEP treatment alleviated some of the safety and transmission concerns between sexually active HIV-negative and HIV-positive men. Within the GMC, the possibility of PrEP offered added protection to HIV-negative gay men who wanted less worry about contracting HIV specifically; compliance with PrEP therapy, which later included other medications besides Truvada, such as the derivative Descovy as well as several injectables, also mitigated concerns somewhat for those who elected not to use condoms as sole protection from transmitting or contracting HIV infection.

Feeling the angst of *I'm almost positive* is still present for some gay men but is significantly reduced after the introduction of more effective treatments, use of PrEP, and markedly fewer HIV diagnoses, as well as notably less incidence of AIDS or deaths from HIV and AIDS. HIV status remains on the radar screen for some gay men as they summarize their valuation of other gay men or themselves. Gay men of different ages and generations will have varied experiences and reactions in relation to HIV and AIDS.

> *HIV status remains on the radar screen for some gay men as they summarize their valuation of other gay men or themselves.*

Feeling like a have-not means feeling inadequate based on unnecessary comparison to other gay men. Some HIV-positive gay men may still feel ashamed and deficient.[44] HIV-positive gay men must overcome or manage any lingering resentment, envy, or idealization of HIV-negative gay men or even of unaffected heterosexual men. The consequences of maintaining critical judgments about HIV-positive gay men will complicate the ability to deflect feelings of being a have-not. Furthermore, HIV has a different meaning for most gay men compared to straight men, especially those who lived through the AIDS crisis of the 1980s and into the 1990s.

PART IV

Characterological Consequences and the Narcissistic Spectrum in the Gay Male Community

CHAPTER 14

Narcissism in the GMC

Some misconceptions surround the definitions and interpretations of narcissist and narcissism. The term *narcissism* is typically understood to describe someone who is vain, self-centered, shallow, and sometimes dramatic. While these traits or features may or may not be associated with a clinically diagnosed narcissistic personality type or disorder, there are additional complex components and clinical criteria to interpret when considering pathological narcissism.

In Greek mythology, Narcissus was a stunning hunter who was also reputedly known for being superficially overconfident. He became obsessed with his own reflection in a pond but was unaware that it was only a manifestation of himself. Narcissus was so mesmerized by his own reflecting image that he literally fell in love with it. His nemesis was drawing him to the water and to himself, which became a paradoxical double-binding punishment for being an arrogant narcissist.

The term *narcissism* describes the manifestation of having an alluring enthrallment with oneself and a profound dismissiveness about others. A narcissistic person is deficient in their ability to truly empathize with others. Those prone to narcissism and more severe variations are typically limited in their ability to cultivate a functional intimate relationship. The story reveals that Narcissus loved himself, but his self-absorption did not allow others to love him back. He despised those who loved him, instead finding himself in a pathological dilemma.

Narcissistic Behaviors, Traits, and Characteristics Versus a More Serious Disorder

You've Been Blocked is not intended to provide an extensive exposé on the subject of narcissism or one that discusses narcissism in a clinically comprehensive manner. However, as I explain here, I believe an elevated level of narcissistic tendency exists in the GMC.

The phenomenon of narcissism and its development is a complex subject when assessing dynamics in the GMC. The higher prevalence of narcissism and related dispositions is likely connected to a unique history for gay men; they often suffer from low self-esteem and are subjected to troubling events during their childhood and adolescent development.[45] Chronically low self-esteem does not automatically lead to narcissism, but it is associated with various mental health conditions like mood disorders, anxiety disorders, addictions, and personality disorders.

Gay men face an arrested development during childhood that blocks critical parts of their true selves in what seems like a permanent or indefinite unresolvable scenario at the time. This blocking-induced sense of emotional and spiritual shutdown sends some gay boys retreating inward; it is layered on top of external reinforcers that often send negative, demeaning messages to gay boys and teens during impressionable time periods. For some, this process is a silent but destructive starting point for the development of elevated narcissistic tendencies. Years of missing out, combined with being restricted, damaged, and feeling undeserving brings out a higher potential for narcissistic traits, features, or less frequently, more severe pathology later on into their adulthood.

Narcissism is associated with several predictable traits and circumstances, with each characteristic or trait being a variation of the other qualities but not necessarily part of a disorder. These more pathological versions of narcissism potentially consist of all or several of the following traits, symptoms, and behaviors:

- **Lacks empathy** or has limited empathy
- **Dismissive** toward others
- **Lacks insight**/doesn't care anyway
- **Insensitive** or callous
- **Shallow**, superficial, phony, elitist, aloof
- **Manipulative**, opportunistic, sometimes attention-seeking
- **Selfish**, self-serving
- **Nonreciprocating**, noncomplimentary
- **Arrogant**, pretentious, elitist, superior
- **Grandiose** and overly self-impressed
- **Embellishes**, brags, or lies
- **Tells stories** that don't make sense
- **Aloof**, cold, indifferent, condescending

Personality Disorders and the *DSM-5-TR*

The Diagnostic and Statistical Manual of Mental Disorders (5th ed., text rev. DSM-5-TR) is a reference guide published by the American Psychiatric Association (APA). It is the official publication that contains the current, recognized diagnostic categories and required criteria used to determine the presence of hundreds of documented psychiatric disorders such as depression, anxiety, and many more. The current edition, *DSM-5-TR*, was updated in 2022 and designates ten specific personality disorders on page 733, which it defines as:

> *An enduring pattern of inner experience and behavior that deviates markedly from the norms and expectations of the individual's culture, is pervasive and inflexible, has an onset in*

adolescence or early adulthood, is stable over time, and leads to distress or impairment.[46]

The *DSM-5-TR* suggests these disorders reflect a pattern that may be manifested in terms of cognition, affect, interpersonal functioning, or impulse control.

Complex conditions are a consequence or a result of several underlying causes and origins. A condition may be diagnosed by mental health professionals as a personality disorder through a process. Clinicians formulate an analytic picture that includes a combination of factors in addition to utilizing a list of specific criteria as stated in the DSM; they are also assessing for elements such as childhood trauma, a likelihood of abuse, and genetic, organic elements that factor into an overall clinical impression.

Dramatic Personality Traits or Features

The APA has categorized personality disorders into three different groups or "clusters" with similar traits. *You've Been Blocked* focuses primarily on Cluster B disorders, which are referred to here as the *narcissistic spectrum*. They "are taxonomically grouped together because a single, clear-cut diagnosis is not always indicated, and patients often exhibit a number of overlapping symptoms."[47] The theme and premise of Cluster B are understood by clinicians and are referred to in the *DSM-5-TR* as *dramatic types*.

Why There May Be a Higher Incidence of the Narcissistic Spectrum in the GMC

Sexual orientation minorities, including gay men, are more prone to mental health issues, including personality disorders.[48]

> **A BRIEF DESCRIPTION OF CLUSTER B PERSONALITY DISORDERS, ALSO REFERRED TO HERE AS THE NARCISSISTIC SPECTRUM**
>
> » **Narcissistic personality disorder (NPD):** deficient ability to empathize with others; more severe egocentrism, opportunism, and calculated selfishness.
>
> » **Antisocial personality disorder (APD):** also known as being a sociopath: inability to feel remorse and authentic regard for rights of others. Many are potentially charming, manipulating, and good actors.
>
> » **Borderline personality disorder (BPD):** basic identity crisis of self; engaging in erratic relationships, severe "splitting" between idealism and devaluation of others. Borderlines are sometimes unclear about self-identity, including sexual identity, gender identity, sexual orientation, and overall personal expression.
>
> » **Histrionic personality disorder (HPD):** drama and problems with emotional regulation/assessing depth of relationships; profoundly lacking intimacy. Histrionics may be overly reactive when they really don't know what they're talking about and likely really don't care.

Consider the influence of being blocked, oppressed, judged, and targeted by society; these create a higher incidence of narcissistic spectrum traits and behaviors in the GMC. It begs the question of whether gay men are prone to narcissistic personality traits and disorders as a compounding consequence of generally elevated levels of childhood blocking, abuse, social subjugation, and ostracization. In other words, gay men may be more prone to narcissistic behaviors, traits, or personality disorders not because they are gay, but because of a systemically influenced negative response by society *to their gayness.*

Mental health professionals such as psychiatrists, psychotherapists, social workers, and psychologists are clinically trained about personality disorders like NPD or other similar disorders. Some of the general public may have heard references or media mentions of various examples such as borderline personality, or others, like antisocial personality, sometimes referred to as "sociopathy" or "psychopathy." Narcissistic personality disorder may be referred to more broadly as narcissism, although NPD is a very specific diagnosis that references more than a general sense of narcissism.

All Cluster B disorders (NPD, APD, BPD, and HPD) have a narcissistic component; they also tend to involve some degree of drama-related chaos. *You've Been Blocked* refers to the Cluster B grouping as the *narcissistic spectrum*, a range of narcissistic traits that affect some gay men who may be infrequently diagnosed with a full personality disorder. It is more likely the case that gay men who have some narcissistic tendencies also display various traits and characteristics found on the narcissistic spectrum (rather than having one particular full-blown clinical characterological diagnosis like NPD). Nonetheless, these Cluster B traits have destructive implications and, particularly for gay men, are usually a product of a history of varied abusive and dysfunctional experiences.

> Cluster B traits have destructive implications and, particularly for gay men, are usually a product of a history of varied abusive and dysfunctional experiences.

Cluster B disorders often compromise the ability to accurately perceive self and others. The various Cluster B disorders are closely related in multiple ways; they share traits, themes, or characteristics with the other Cluster B disorders but have distinct qualities that set each one apart from the others.

Varied forms and the extent of an abuse history or other damage often factor into the narcissistic spectrum. This can include how traumatized the person was in childhood and the type of historical (child) sexual, physical, psychological, or emotional abuse or damage that occurred. Sometimes the abuse, especially mental abuse, can be particularly insidious in notably dysfunctional families. Vile sexual or physical abuse during childhood makes mental health issues, including personality disorders, more likely in adulthood. This historical trauma can potentially impact functions of adequate empathy, remorse, maintaining appropriate boundaries, and emotional regulation in adults. Someone diagnosed with NPD may also exhibit behavior traits similar to those displayed in the other three disorders in the cluster or spectrum although the main impression meets more specific criteria for NPD.

For example, the classic antisocial personality disorder (APD) trait of deficient remorse as well as unashamed disregard for rights or feelings of others intersects with limited empathy noted in narcissism and NPD, but it is seen more succinctly and more often in APD. In borderline personality disorder (BPD), volatile relationships and an unstable sense of self are the main symptoms, but compromised functions of empathy, remorse, and emotional self-control are also present. Sometimes, dramatic behavior and traits are trivialized or made out to be amusing but are more a part of damaged, dysfunctional, overly emotional, and hyperreactive, melodramatic gay men; in their more pathological versions, they are part of histrionic personality disorder (HPD).

Histrionics and dramatic behavior—or simply put, "drama"—are concentrated and primarily part of HPD, but they are also routinely seen in all four of the Cluster B disorders. Independent of stereotypes and campy comic relief, gay men in the GMC can facilitate and perpetuate a dramatic sensationalized spectacle at times. This may seem entertaining and potentially humorous, but the melodramatics undermine healthy relationships. This unstable behavior is not well received among other, more emotionally stable gay men. Histrionics feed negative stereotypes about sometimes unhinged gay men acting out, particularly with the normalization of these antics depicted on social media.

Higher Incidence of Narcissism and Related Personality Disorders and Traits in Gay Men

One of the primary reasons that the narcissistic spectrum may be more prevalent among gay men is related to a faulty, invalidating response from an external environment consisting mainly of heterosexual presumption, including parents, family, and school. Gay boys can become confused, scared, and uncertain; they are rightfully unsure how to respond to a conflict between what and who they authentically are and what they think they are supposed to be, in response to the expectations of others.

> *Gay boys can become confused, scared, and uncertain; they are rightfully unsure how to respond to a conflict between what and who they authentically are and what they think they are supposed to be, in response to expectations of others.*

DYSFUNCTIONAL FOUNDATIONS OF EACH PERSONALITY TRAIT AND DISORDER AS PART OF A SPECTRUM: HOW THEY MIGHT PLAY OUT AND BE RELEVANT TO GAY MEN

- » Higher exposure to mixed messages, invalidation, identity confusion, and volatile abuse/home environments = **borderline/borderlining**

- » History of keeping secrets, lying, stringent perfection-seeking, pressure to overaccommodate and take care of others = backlash later on: **narcissism and antisocial (sociopathy)**

- » Compartmentalizing identities, repressing sexuality, manipulating, suppressing remorse and emotions = **antisocial/sociopathic**

- » Melodramatic, phony acting routines, including feeling forced to act straight when really gay, plus displaying dramatic inappropriate reactions in various capacities and scenarios (sometimes seen in *allegedly* closeted celebrities) = **histrionics**

The *DSM-5-TR* states that approximately 2–3% of the general population may plausibly be diagnosed with one of 10 personality disorders. I believe the prevalence of NPD, the narcissistic spectrum, or similar traits and disorders is likely higher for gay men than in the general population.

Gay men are prone to experience inconsistent or invalidating, intolerant support systems; this is coupled with an internalized, private, secretive, shameful conclusion that questions their sexual identity. Identity chaos leads to a higher likelihood of narcissism and other neuroses as gay adults. Some gay boys and gay men develop a protective, egocentric arrogance to compensate for these inadequacies. A history of inconsistent messages, abuse, shaming, and devaluing is a risk factor for developing aspects of the narcissistic spectrum.[49]

Risk Factors Associated with the Narcissistic Spectrum Include Nurture and Nature

Certain life experiences (nurture) during childhood create an increased risk for developing personality disorders as adults. This exposure is combined with genetic (nature), emotional, or psychological predispositions. The severity and impact of these factors encompass a range of abuse, neglect, and inappropriate parenting. Rigid or fluid boundaries and hereditary factors such as family history of personality disorders, addictions, or other mental health conditions may also be present.

> *Certain life experiences (nurture) during childhood create an increased risk for developing personality disorders as adults.*

Nature/Nurture: Genetics Plus Damage and Injury

Emerging gay male children face unique challenges because of their profound differences. They are impacted by the reactions of parents, family, and community environments like home and school settings. A gay boy's normalcy is quite different and usually not what their parents had anticipated.

Many gay men do not grow up being and feeling accepted for who they are; they are subjected to an unnecessary, violating identity crisis that can later develop into a higher likelihood of personality problems and, less frequently, personality disorders.

Biologically based risk factors (nature) contribute to the development of personality disorders or related features/traits. Additionally, individuals who are diagnosed with personality disorders typically were seriously impacted or "injured" emotionally and psychologically by environmental influences; this may include exposure to extensive abuse. A greater abuse history creates a higher risk for the development of personality disorders later on.

Perfection-Seeking and the Need for Reconciling a History of Invalidation

The actions and attitudes of perfection-seeking behavior are seen as part of narcissistic personality traits or disorders.[50] In line with NPD criteria of seeking perfectionism, gay men sometimes have a fantasy about finding ideal love; some feel they should only be connected to a certain caliber of person (date/mate/man to be with) or institution/brand/employer. Narcissists sometimes define their fragile sense of self through who or what they associate with, either by seeking it out or attempting to be sought after in some regard. For gay men, narcissistic tendencies likely stem from earlier experiences of deficient validation and identification because of being different; as adults, they are highly prone to an adolescent-style need to be associated with a certain group. Sometimes the cliques consist of other distressed, approval-seeking gay men.

> *Narcissists sometimes define their fragile sense of self through who or what they associate with.*

Identity Confusion, Crisis, and Disorders

Gay men grow up in environments that foster a high potential for experiencing an unclear sense of self. For example, confusion of sexual identity is one notable trait seen in the related Cluster B diagnosis, borderline personality disorder (BPD). Becoming aware of a gay sexual orientation and then eventually having to identify as gay creates a higher risk and strains a more discernible identity development. Unlike a straight male, a gay man must maneuver through an involved process to determine, understand, and somehow accept their very different, often criticized sexuality.

Sometimes, borderline personality traits or features are displayed when gay men insist they are supposedly bisexual or experiencing disruptive confusion of sexual preference. Perhaps for some, perpetual sexual identity/orientation unsureness is better accounted for as either closeted homosexuality with or without borderline traits or disorders rather than consistently attributing the fluidity to identifying as bisexual.

A history of inadequate validation in childhood is a predictable component in adult personality difficulties and disorders.[51] When gay boys are inhibited from being themselves, many are inclined to downplay who they are, making attempts to self-portray as straight-normal. This can leave them less likely to receive a normal, comparable level of basic validation for who they really are, which results in fundamental damage to their core foundation of self.

Anxiety

A tangled combination of anxiety, depression, and an unstable sense of self is complicated by identity confusion and interpersonal problems. The inconsistent or conditional acceptance and blocking history can elevate anxiety and depression. Conditional acceptance leaves gay boys feeling on edge, worrying about what might happen next. Many feel ambivalent about whether they are a good person or not, if they are right or wrong, if they are immoral, and if they are normal and sane or abnormal and crazy.

Trauma and Abuse in Various Forms

Many gay boys inevitably experience trauma after years of being socially ostracized and shamed. Traumatic childhood experience is associated with a higher risk for the development of more severe mental health conditions, which sometimes include personality disorders.[52] Young, developing gay boys may be more sensitive or sexually precocious and curious; other times, they may be more guarded, defensive, and homophobic, so some will act out aggressively and incur erratic or abusive interactions with other peers or adults.

Gay male children are more likely to be victimized by those older than them, including predatory adults, some of whom may be latent/closeted male homosexuals; the abusers sense that gay boys are different and see them as vulnerable targets. In addition to family and extended family, examples of possible predators and boundary violators include those hiding behind religious affiliations and other comparable authority figures.

Abnormal Stress Levels

"Various forms of early life adversity, particularly experiences of abuse and neglect, portend the development of personality disorders and maladaptive personality traits later in life."[53] Stress is elevated because a gay boy's framework for a version of authentic normalcy is not the same experience of "normal" that straight boys have; this originates from home, school, religious, and general social environmental pressures. Gay boys are subjected to constant scrutiny and worry about alleged or actual gayness or gay traits emerging; many gay boys are anxious about being harassed, outed, attacked, and shamed.

> *Some gay boys are afraid to speak openly in public or social settings for fear of being shamed.*

Some gay boys are afraid to speak openly in public or social settings for fear of being shamed; their fears are understandable and based on past experiences when society and their own parents reacted negatively to signs of gayness. The stress and anxiety are reinforced before, during, and after the unpleasant interactions.

Bullying and "Mobbing"

Gay boys are routinely victims of perpetual and targeted abuse and bullying. Less frequently, they may become the bully, someone who projects their identity crisis, low self-worth, and self-loathing onto other peers; they will sometimes subjugate others, but many still feel deeply insecure and full of self-loathing or identity confusion. When gay boys are bullied, they shut down emotionally with a dangerous combination of self-loathing and a pervasive sense of shame. Severe bullying or conditional acceptance in childhood can lead to suicide attempts, sometimes with tragic results.

> When gay boys are bullied, they shut down emotionally with a dangerous combination of self-loathing and a pervasive sense of shame.

Larger scale, collective, and sensationalized attacks by specific groups are called *mobbing*. There may be improvements in awareness and interception of bullying and more systemically overtly openly anti-gay attacks. However, for many decades, it was common for an entire organization, such as a student body at a school (or a collective anti-gay perspective from mainstream society), to target gay boys or gay men by supporting a merciless, widespread general and/or specific anti-gay hate campaign. These incursions can become layered from multiple external sources, such as from other religious or political groups, parts of society/other communities, or even certain regions where anti-gay momentum flourishes. Internationally, there are numerous countries with fundamentalist religious influence that support extreme government control; some governments have laws where being "caught" being gay is legally enforced and sometimes results in corporal punishment, incarceration, and/or execution.[54] Discrimination in different capacities against gay men is likely to continue in certain societies, communities, and countries regardless of laws or political and social pressures or improvements in the Western world or larger more progressive cities.

Mobbing is a collective bullying technique that has fueled multiple examples of institutionalized hate and discrimination. The crimes against humanity committed during the Holocaust of the 1930s and 1940s is a classic example of how mobbing is used to create a pervasive, toxic response. Mobbing continues to be used more than ever today on all media, including social media, as a method to politicize and "gaslight" to facilitate a sweeping response. Mobbing has negatively impacted certain groups, including gay men, over many years, thanks to propaganda and sensationalism.

There has been an apparent spike in mobbing-related sensationalism both domestically and internationally, with a notable increase after 2008, when there was amplified focus on "identity politics." This increase appears to further coincide with the controversial aspects of the COVID-19 pandemic, significant social and political events, and a surge in polarized political discourse.

After years of being real or actual victims of mobbing, some gay men respond with what looks like a campaign for social justice on behalf of gays and other groups. Some of these efforts may be well intended. However, in other cases, the response consists of spewing negative, biased views that are not accurate or helpful to gay people —or anybody, particularly not other minorities. It amounts to more of an affected projection of victimhood and inadequacy than a genuine, constructive concern for underdogs or true empathetic tolerance of their fellow gay men or other marginalized groups. Gay men will not respond positively to insidious persecution, so their reactions are sometimes reflective of their triggered, personal history of being subjugated and blocked.

Substance Abuse

Elevated substance abuse is a common factor in the narcissistic spectrum. Drugs, alcohol, food, sex, spending, codependency, and similar addictions and behaviors begin as short-term coping mechanisms. A young, developing gay boy/adolescent may be driven to test limits prematurely and more intrepidly than their straight peers with drugs and alcohol or related compulsive/addictive behaviors.[55] Gay boys may be acting out and exposed to substance abuse and compulsive behaviors at younger ages than straight boys. Because social ostracization provoked their anxiety, gay boys are more apt to be oppositional and experiment with drugs and "adult themes."[56] Substance abuse is then later reinforced and normalized in parts of the social dynamics of the GMC.

Environmental Dynamics in the GMC Are Conducive to Narcissistic Tendencies

Cynical gay men can create a synergistic effect in the GMC, and some of them may not be particularly shocked by the elevated prevalence of narcissistic behavior. From that starting point, egocentrism, also known as self-absorption, can exacerbate a more serious narcissism among some gay men by normalizing its presence as part of the dynamics in the GMC. Gay men tend to experience a lifestyle that is more prone to self-focused patterns compared to their heterosexual contemporaries.[57] Gay men are more likely to be single and childless compared to straight men. It makes sense, in this case, that they comparatively tend to have more disposable income than straight men overall. Gay men may be more available and interested in catering to their various personal needs and self-fulfilling desires compared to straight men. Having more disposable income and

> Gay men may be more available and interested in catering to their various personal needs and self-fulfilling desires compared to straight men.

related lifestyle implications does not make someone a narcissist, but having greater access to resources and socially reinforced environmental and lifestyle factors are relative to some increased risk for narcissistic *tendencies*.

If a gay man is not narcissistic or especially egocentric, it is still likely that he will engage with other gay men who are prone to some element or symptomology of narcissism. It is narcissistic to conceptualize about falling in love with the perfect man. Some are imagining a mirror image of themselves or a sense of pressure to *become* this idealized image. They are in love with themselves, so to speak.

Mental Health and Genetics

Various genetic (biologically based) predispositions to mental illness pose an added layer of dysfunction. Some parents and families exhibit mental illness as well as modeling emotionally unstable behaviors.

Some gay boys may have parents who are troubled individuals or, other times, latent homosexuals who have serious blockage issues, including acknowledgment and acceptance of their own sexual identity. They may suffer from untreated mental health conditions, such as depression or unresolved, abuse histories. Gay men sometimes learn that one of their parents or siblings is gay and quite possibly a repressed homosexual.

Gayness Runs in the Family

It is not uncommon for gay men to have a gay sibling or parent. Some gay male clients have described scenarios where they have an immediate family member, either a sibling or a parent, who they suspect or learn is gay and/or closeted. Even more damaging is when a closeted parent flips their self-loathing around in a noxious way that projects and displaces their self-hatred onto their own gay son. Any latent gay tendencies in a gay boy's parent, particularly the

> *It is not uncommon for gay men to have a gay sibling or parent.*

father, can be further exacerbated by having a triggering gay son. Comparatively, the gay son is more often eventually out of the closet and more openly gay. This can infuriate a closeted father who, for example, because of *repressed* homosexuality, may project abusive homophobia onto the gay son.

Detachment

Some gay men may come to feel decreased concern for others, including other gay men; they may feel they've done more than their share of pleasing others after being blocked and violated for many years. Being single and uncommitted sometimes reinforces a narcissistic core, perhaps related to the primal origins of male survival. Some gay men will be naturally inclined to be and live alone in their own private world and grow accustomed to it.

This detachment is part of another reinforcing layer of a narcissistic sense of existence. Some of those who end up unattached and perpetually single are displeased with their detachment and disconcerted about why they can't develop functional, intimate connections with other gay men like they *think* they want to.

There are gay men who are genuinely dissatisfied with their lack of attachment; there are others who are content being single, as well as those who need to accept that they don't really want or need this type of connection or may not be well-suited for it.

CRITICAL THINKING CHOICE CHECKPOINT #16

The narcissistic spectrum may encompass various indicators, traits, and features seen in "Cluster B personality disorders." Behavior traits can include any part or combination of factors, like deficient empathy, compromised sense of remorse, and overly dramatic volatile relationships.

CHAPTER 15

Identity Confusion, Disorders, and Narcissism in Gay Men

Identity refers to qualities, beliefs, personality, visual characteristics, and expressions that make a person or group who or what they are. Some of the essential elements that compose identity development include sexual identity, which includes sexual orientation (who you are attracted to romantically and/or sexually).

The early years and stages of child development comprise a critical period for all young children. Any child, regardless of sexual orientation, can potentially struggle or be confused about their sense of self. However, gay boys are more likely to become distressed and challenged about their identity and sense of self.[58] Gay boys must encounter and address an emerging homosexual identity; this process is more complex, more confusing for some, and often deterred or criticized. Their straight peers will not experience or relate to this marked difference in identity development.

Blocking gay boys during their formidable childhood years creates ambiguity that can lead to an identity disturbance. As children, feeling or being threatened by a shame-based, hostile external environment can perpetuate an identity crisis. Even if younger, preadolescent gay boys develop some juvenile awareness of what may be different about them, they may not be fully able to generate a constructive, open conversation at the time about exactly *what* that differentness means.

The Effects of Childhood Identity Confusion on Adult Gay Men

Gay men may have more clarity about identity as adults *because they are adults*. Many gay men understand that they must deconstruct the detrimental effects of childhood identity confusion. They have to reprogram learned faulty messages, along with reclaiming underdeveloped, blocked parts of themselves. This requires a reboot after being subjected to expectations that they should be something they are not.

Some may begin to realize that their "identity confusion" is mainly a function of negative reinforcements based on how they are received by parents and peers. Additional challenges arise because identity is supposed to happen organically, so adult gay men play "catch-up" because this is not developed at a time-sensitive juncture.

Other obstacles may occur when gay men are not mindful that they have deeper work to do on themselves, besides going to the gym, to reestablish a solid sense of self. Some may require more exploration than others in reclaiming their identity; some believe they have resolved their identity confusion based solely on coming out of the closet. This is a point where they may determine their self-improvement consists of how they look and, for some, how not-gay they appear (such as amplifying their M-Ranking market value). This is a similar reenactment from childhood people-pleasing and fabricating an ill-fitting, inauthentic identity. Many now find themselves pandering to some perceived need for approval from other gay men.

> *As children, many gay men will have difficulty developing an authentic identity if they do not experience natural, normal, unrestricted evolving milestones equal to those of their straight peers.*

Connections Among Identity Development, Identity Disorders, and Personality Disorders

> **GAY MEN AND IDENTITY DISORDERS IN CHILDHOOD AND PERSONALITY DISORDERS INTO ADULTHOOD**
>
> » 🔹 Gay boys are more likely to be violated and blocked from being themselves. 🔹
>
> » 🔹 This may lead to a higher incidence of developmental identity problems growing up. 🔹
>
> » 🔹 A higher incidence of developmental identity problems in childhood equals a higher incidence for personality problems and disorders in adulthood. 🔹
>
> » 🔹 Bottom Line: Based on this descriptive chain of development, adult gay men are then more prone to mental health issues, including personality disorders in some rarer instances.

Recall that gay boys are commonly validated for who they are *not* rather than as a basic, standard, unmitigated acknowledgment of who they *are*. The abnormal childhood process of responding to pressure to identify inauthentically may have a synergistic impact on blocking a gay man's true self; this creates identity confusion and chaos. For example, in some cases, a history of trauma and identity issues contributes to a higher risk for borderline personality disorder (BPD) later in adult relationships.[59] Personality problems or disorders may develop after a history of identity disturbance in childhood.[60]

Gay boys will predictably encounter more difficulty in developing a clear sense of insight, self, and identity. After feeling persistently insecure, some gay boys tend to retreat inward, which can set up a narcissistic pathway. Life experience builds upon a continuous, progressive accumulation. Being blocked causes considerable delays or omissions; some experience arrested development with subsequent milestones often times not adequately met.

The Leap from Anxiety and Confusion to Personality Disorders

Identity development is critical at many life stages during childhood, and a link exists among identity development, sexual identity, identity disorders, and personality disorders. Basically, a history of significant identity problems and complications, plus related dysfunction and disorders in childhood, creates a higher risk for mental health issues and neuroses, like personality problems/disorders, into adolescence and adulthood.[61]

It is crucial, especially during adolescence, that children are allowed to naturally explore identity development. Some gay boys will be negatively affected even when they appear to be confident and stabilized with more family support.

Conundrum of Celebration Versus Subjugation

Gay boys sometimes feel caught in a mixed trap of being reactive, dramatic, and histrionic. Others become egocentric, emotionally closed off, shut down, or insensitive, with compromised remorse (sometimes sociopathic in nature).

This imbalance of hypersensitivity and being overly empathetic versus insensitive and egocentric leads to confusion or a superimposed "dis-orientation." This is another point where retreating inward is intensified, becoming a potential predisposition for the development of narcissism.

This egocentric retreat inward is a paradoxical method to self-protect and self-preserve. The irony is that the narcissistic qualities are often the psyche's response to regulating a sense of severe insecurity and traumatic experience. For some gay men, this stems from deficient, low self-esteem. This may explain how some of the most seemingly beautiful, sexy, popular gay men, models, celebrities, and alleged closeted celebrities secretly feel like they are also some of the most insecure and miserable impostors.

CHAPTER 16

Defense Mechanisms and Delusions

Being in a state of denial blocks authenticity. For gay men, a state of denial and blocking is based on years of perfected technique through childhood, which can create additional unblocking work to be done into adulthood.

Defense Mechanisms

The psychoanalytic theory proposed by Dr. Sigmund Freud identified unconscious, subconscious, and conscious actions and defenses humans engage in to safeguard various unpleasant emotions like anxiety, insecurity, or self-loathing.[62] Freudian defenses play a critical role as protective functions activated by young gay boys to cope with blocking their sexual identity. The defense mechanisms are commonly seen at different junctures throughout their lives.

Denial

Denial is the basic defense. Most gay boys commonly block out and negate their gayness by *denying* who they are.

Defense mechanisms impede various natural progressions. For example, many gay boys feel pressured to represent a straight-normal image; they try to temporarily avoid conflict by appeasing their parents and general society. Tentatively deflecting attention offers some protective function rather than risk immediate judgment and punitive consequences for revealing gayness.

Gay men are distressed when faced with a sense of urgency to act as though they're interested in something they are not. Other times they must resist and deny their genuine interest in something that they *are* or would be genuinely interested in or yearning for, such as same sex-attraction.

Repression

Similar to denial, *repression* allows for certain memories, emotions, feelings, desires, or impulses to be essentially "pushed" into the unconscious memory. Freud's theory suggests humans self-protect by repressing or blocking unpleasant drives and emotions, including abusive pasts. As a result, the psyche would not be permeated immediately. This temporary protective process enables some degree of emotional functioning, despite the effects of a potentially traumatic situation.

Problems resurfacing as repressed memories either become less repressible or something triggers them to release again. It is tempting for gay men to avoid and hide from frightening feelings. Their true self is often hidden and shut off, but it is still present, even if it is just under the surface. The gay sexual orientation is not going away, regardless of temporary or ongoing repression efforts.

Compartmentalization and Sociopathy

Many gay boys encounter trauma and confusion when they begin to realize something feels different or that they *are* different or gay. This reality provokes fear of how others, especially parents and peers, will react to them. They learn to temporarily become something they are not by sealing off parts of themselves. Eventually, many will make some attempt to come out. However, in the meantime, their identity is often *compartmentalized* through closing off the assorted pieces and variations of themselves.

Gay men *compensate* for their deficiencies at times by overextending or impeding themselves in various ways. Sometimes this is revealed as overachievement (overcompensation). Other times, this may involve underachievement or choosing to be associated with "lower companions." Gay boys often compensate to make their inauthentic, contrived lives feel more bearable. This way, they can complement their level of denial and repression.

Many gay boys may then opt to intermittently or partially unseal different parts of themselves, depending on various interactions and the junctures and ages of their development. The more extreme, pathological version of compartmentalization can include aspects of sociopathy, also known as antisocial personality disorder (APD). *Sociopathy* is an extreme variation of compartmentalizing that restricts emotional reaction. Pathological lying about actions and events that proceeded, including minimizing gay sexual identity or sexual activity that took place, is a classic indication of sociopathic behavioral traits. Sometimes, particularly for closeted or "down-low" (DL) men, perhaps a gay sexual encounter happens, but some will act like it never transpired; it's as though they try to make something uncomfortable seamlessly disappear or never exist in the first place.

Sociopathic traits and behaviors are displayed by people who have an ability to be a certain way, do a certain behavior, and then act like the behavior never happened; they may fool themselves and also outwardly suggest, "It wasn't me." The main feature seen in those diagnosed with antisocial personality disorder (APD) is a profound lack of remorse, which also allows for a drastic separation of various "compartments" as needed to manipulate or convince others.

More serious compartmentalization allows for some gay men to almost split off and adopt different personas as needed. Some gay men find it acceptable to disrespect other gay men; they can be nasty, cutting, and disregarding of the rights of others, but then minimize their actions and the impact of their nastiness to other gay men as if it didn't happen. Some of those engaging in this behavior are delusional enough to think they are not acting in this offensive manner at all; others can be grandiose in thinking they are actually thoughtful humanitarians, even when they're acting out in an offensive or dismissive manner to others, particularly other gay men.

Compensation

People-pleasing is a familiar and well-learned form of compensation and a defense undertaken by gay boys and gay men to gratuitously accommodate others. For example, when parents, peers, teachers, coworkers, or friends are feared to be "uncomfortable" with the idea of homosexuality and gayness, gay boys often feel obligated to repress and shut off their gayness and true selves. Gay boys respond by formulating a distinctive message that says, "You must like me; I must make you like me, accept me, and make everything look okay."

Lower self-worth and desperate approval-seeking lead some gay boys to erroneously internalize the notion that they must be liked by other people. They begin to incorrectly conclude that they have to do anything necessary to essentially make everything okay or better for everyone else. They don't want to be too offensive to those they fear may have a problem with gay men. Perhaps this is one reason why some gay men are skilled at making aesthetics and images like hair styling, makeup, clothing, and interior design look so pristine. This dynamic frequently becomes *codependency,* when the care and concern for others—like parents, coworkers, or peers and relationships—is prioritized in lieu of genuine self-care. Feeling resentment or rage is also commonly associated with this type of codependent people-pleasing; this is a disastrous precursor for dysfunctional adult relationships, including various blocked, intimate connections with other gay men.

Projection and Displacement

The defense mechanism of *projection* comes into play when we rationalize our own feelings or issues as though the other person, rather than ourselves, has the problem or issue. Those who project will accuse another person of doing, feeling, or being what they are themselves.

After childhood years of being repeatedly disrespected by others, and likely being victims of other dysfunctional people projecting their issues on to them, gay men have a higher tendency for self-hatred; they may be inclined to outwardly project these negative sentiments onto others who remind them of themselves. Some gay men target other gay men as well; projecting is one way gay men reduce anxiety, insecurity, and personal discomfort; it involves accusing or blaming others or attributing one's own emotions, traits, or problems to others. Projecting is a passive-aggressive, self-righteous defense mechanism. It is a tactic that is frequently present throughout social media and sensationalized mainstream media and political arenas. Political parties are collectively experts at projecting, including the idea and accusation that opposing parties are the ones projecting.

Disturbing feelings like guilt, fear, shame, and rage may be temporarily reduced by accusing or blaming someone or something else. Gay men, especially repressed, latent (closeted) homosexuals or those confused or "questioning," sometimes see another gay man acting in a way they personally disapprove of that makes them uncomfortable. Being exposed in this fashion can elicit an unpleasant, disapproving, self-loathing type of emotional reaction for some gay men.

A classic example occurs when closeted or latent homosexuals *project* their internal discomfort, internalized homophobia, and self-hatred outward; they react in a nasty, critical, destructive way to protect themselves. This is especially relevant when they observe someone who might appear to fit certain stereotypical perceptions of their negative impressions of a gay or effeminate man. The fundamental idea behind projecting is that the person must relieve a sense of discomfort with their own issues by accusing, abusing, or blaming others.

With *displacement*, disturbing emotions, like anger or resentment at someone or something, are redirected or transferred and focused onto someone or something else. Gay boys being bullied and harassed at school are known to act out at home, or they will bully someone or something else. Sometimes, closeted homosexuals or other insecure adults project and displace their own inner disturbance, conflict, and self-hatred onto others; gay boys or adult gay men are frequent targets, especially if the discomfort pertains to gay sexuality matters.

Reaction Formation

The American Psychological Association (APA) defines *reaction formation* as "a defense mechanism in which unacceptable or threatening unconscious impulses are denied and are replaced in consciousness with their opposite."[63] Reaction formation is a specific systemic type of projection and includes elements of other defense mechanisms, such as denial, avoidance, repression, displacement, and compensation. In reaction formation, most of the defenses are integrated to some degree to create a self-protective façade. Some gay men put up a front to cover their anxiety-producing underlying emotional triggers.

A common version of reaction formation is seen when closeted homosexuals make a valiant effort to be outwardly heterosexual. For some closeted homosexuals, this may include negative criticism or more severe threats or hatefulness directed toward gay men. This would sometimes include putting on a dramatic façade, such as attempts to be especially macho, including more crude attention-seeking actions like graphic discussions about sexual acts with women, when they really aren't interested in women at all.

Young children are known to act out reaction formation when they insist and sometimes verbalize how much they hate someone when they may have a crush on them and ostensibly feel quite the opposite. This is an intersection of other defense mechanisms (denying and repressing the truth and reality and projecting it outward to diffuse their own discomfort with their reality). Reaction formation includes dramatic qualities seen in the narcissistic spectrum, like histrionics. Reaction formation is a defense that can quickly become destructive and abusive. The power of reaction formation can lead to a variety of lashing-out behaviors directed at and against other undeserving individuals. Gay men are prone to becoming victims of this type of abuse; sometimes they become perpetrators as well.

Hostile, anti-gay individuals, including sometimes other closeted gay men, seek a passive-aggressive sense of relief in targeting gay men. The anti-gay man who is in the closet himself may be triggered and acting out his self-hatred by abusing and punishing other gay men. Some gay men are exploited by closeted homosexuals in various social settings like school, work, or within families. Gay men can function as unsuspecting victims who elicit some negative response from an insecure external source.

Numerous gay men have reported being targeted by closeted gay men and subjected to deliberate prejudice, particularly in the workplace. These reports consisted of experiences that included slanderous, destructive attacks; the perpetrators were frequently conflicted people who often faced only minimal consequences themselves while the gay boys or gay men were frequently targeted, humiliated, penalized, and blocked some more.

Young heterosexual children might occasionally engage in reaction formation as perpetrator or victim. However, gay boys are more frequently vulnerable because they are easy prey for other bullies. Gay boys are particularly susceptible to being treated unfairly or singled out by those with some personal identity crisis, like angry, infuriated closeted homosexuals or those with some other severe dysfunction in their lives, such as lower IQ, abuse, or feeling like an implicit failure. Some of the more vocal, aggressively anti-gay actions come from anti-gay religious leaders or politicians, who may actually be latent homosexuals; some are deeply closeted, struggling, feeling weak, and terrified of their own sense of personally humiliating homosexual tendencies.

Delusions

Some gay men deny their true selves by creating a *delusion of grandeur* and acting as though they're something spectacular when they are generally quite average. They may also delude themselves into thinking they're better than and more masculine or straight-acting than other gay men, yet many are average at best and/or continue to repress undesired emotions, including insecurity, self-loathing, and any feminine traits/signs of gayness.

Instead of a genuine, authentic display, some gay men present an altered self in a deliberately crafted fashion, even if they are openly gay and out of the closet. They have difficulty with intimacy and various close relationships, so they substitute a contrived, phony persona for their true selves. This dynamic fits in with a Hollywood-type of social climbing. Grandiose delusions are personified in some gay men within the narcissistic spectrum as variations of histrionics, sociopathy, borderlining, or classic narcissism.

CHAPTER 17

Alcoholic Thinking, Alcoholic Behavior, the Pleasure Principle, and Similar Compulsions

Using and abusing substances like drugs and alcohol, binge eating, and being sexually compulsive are significant to many gay men at some point in their lives. Use of alcohol and other substances is woven into the social fabric in the GMC, whether at public bars and events or privately at gatherings or parties. Some feel the need to self-medicate with drugs, alcohol, and other substances to manage stress, social anxiety, and depression.

Seeking pleasure, relief, and socialization through drug and alcohol use is familiar and somewhat encouraged and reinforced in the GMC.[64] Most gay men are *not* alcoholics or addicts. However, "gay and transgender populations experience higher rates of substance use."[65] The 2020 National Survey on Drug Use and Health: Lesbian, Gay, or Bisexual (LGB) Adults, conducted by the Substance Abuse and Mental Health Services Administration (SAMHSA), found that more than 20% of LGBTQ+ adults had an alcohol use disorder within that year. There were also elevated rates of usage of multiple controlled substances and street drugs in the LGBTQ+ community.[66]

Alcoholic Behavior, Mentality, and Attitudes

Untreated is a term that refers to addicts or alcoholics who may or may not be actively using substances or engaging in compulsive behaviors or drinking; most have not had any treatment or recovery. Untreated and/or actively using addicts and alcoholics tend to present a false, ego-based persona with synthetic confidence , especially when they are intoxicated.

Some alcoholic behavior is seen in those who are not using or drinking, yet they are still exhibiting similar thought patterns and behaviors, interacting as though they were actively using. Behaviors and thought patterns associated with and displayed by addicts are referred to as *addict and alcoholic thinking and behavior*. My concept of "alcoholic behavior" is that similar behavior patterns could be displayed with or without the presence of active substance use.

Addictive behaviors and thinking patterns often include profound self-centeredness (narcissism) and disregard for others. Addicts and alcoholics can exhibit erratic behaviors during their addiction and disease. These behaviors and actions can be motivated by an idealistic need to feel good or a certain way all the time.

> Addictive behaviors and thinking patterns often include profound self-centeredness (narcissism) and disregard for others.

Many addicts and alcoholics have difficulty with boundaries and delayed gratification, especially if they want to binge eat, get high or drunk, or feel sexually validated, for example. Other related behaviors are poor impulse control and difficulty tolerating unpleasant emotions.

Alcoholic Behavior and Alcoholic Thinking Create a Mentality That Fuels Self-Centeredness

Alcoholic thinking and behavior imply that the person creates their own reality, which may include personal grandiosity while minimizing the focus on other people. Frequently, untreated addicts or those considered unsober are primarily concerned about their own feelings, their emotions, their needs, their next drink, their next high.

"ALCOHOLIC BEHAVIOR" MANIFESTATIONS MIGHT INCLUDE:

» **Blocking out distress or anxiety:** Substances are required to manage or accompany most situations, supporting a hedonistic belief that "I must feel good all the time."

» **Blurry boundaries:** Where they begin and end is unclear. Intrusion, collusion, avoidance, and codependency are possible.

» **Compensating for low self-worth/insecurity** underneath an altered persona of inauthentic confidence.

» **Grandiosity,** a false sense of arrogance, distorted reality.

» **Impaired judgment from being drunk, high, or under the influence;** having withdrawals; alternating with detoxing or "coming down" and needing to "come up" or get high on various substances, including food and process addictions, like shopping, working, or being addicted to other people/relationships.

» **Impulsivity:** difficulty accepting delayed gratification and sitting with emotional discomfort.

» **Irresponsibility:** lacking follow-through with commitments.

» **Low distress tolerance:** a sense of urgency to swiftly remove unpleasantries.

» **Manipulating,** lying, general dishonesty, and sneaking around.

» **Unrealistic expectations** of self and others.

» **Mixed-message communications:** not clearly making their point, inconsistency, "all over the place."

» **Mood shifts:** constantly changing moods, erratic, irritable, manic, and depressed.

» **Self-centeredness/ignoring others:** ultimately caring the most about self and personal fulfillment; limited empathy.

> **Unpredictable behavior:** fluctuating in and out of other people's lives, depending on mood or how high or drunk they are or feel they want or need to be. "Never know what or who you'll get." Sometimes it's as though you are "talking to the drug" and not the person.

Alcoholic Behavior Plays Out in the GMC

Regular use of recreational substances or alcohol does not automatically indicate the presence of addiction or alcoholism, yet it is a normalized form of social behavior and etiquette in parts of the GMC. It is unclear how aware gay men are about the presence of alcoholic behavior in the GMC. Some gay men maintain that drinking and partying is generally just about having fun. Gay men sometimes become so enmeshed in their regimen of drinking and using that they don't see their own alcoholism; other times, they may overlook or minimize the progression and worsening of what is becoming a serious disease and mental condition. Some do not identify the chaotic behaviors in themselves or others.

Thanks to years of blocking in Dimensions #1 and #2 that sometimes span both childhood and adult periods, some gay men become experts at magical acting and magical thinking, pretending to be something they are not. Some feel inclined to stretch their reality into a more favorable version or a *distorted sense of self*. Substance abuse can perpetuate a pseudo-self and a quasi-reality.

The rationale of an alcoholic mentality or alcoholic personality allows an addict to live in a partial fantasy. Confidence and power can be enhanced by chemically lowering inhibition and maintaining distorted thinking. Substance abuse is common among the narcissistic spectrum symptomology and disorders (including NPD, BPD, APD, HPD).[67] Substance abuse problems and personality disorders are also prevalent among those working in the entertainment industries and higher-profile people, including celebrities.

Alcoholic Behavior Fosters a Process of Pseudo Self-Acceptance

Alcoholic behavior is seen in people with chronically low self-worth who also develop distorted self-perceptions; historically, for self-protection or out of fear of punitive consequences, some gay men feel pressure to remain repressed and inauthentic. After a childhood of blocking, some will use substances like drugs or alcohol to create an assortment of delusions to manage distress. Those who choose to never come out struggle with inauthenticity, which can mimic alcoholic behavior, whether they are actively drinking or using, or not.

Some gay men realize they have an addiction, or they are more aware of their tendency toward addiction or a history of it. Through maturation that may include treatment like 12-step and other recovery programs, they may begin to discern the classic alcoholic/addict behavior in self or others. Recovery and sobriety allow for greater insight into the unflattering, egocentric indicators of alcoholic behavior.

Partying Drives the Gay Male Social Engine

The extensive emphasis some gay men place on alcohol and substance consumption is remarkable. Gay bars have historically been a central cornerstone of the gay male social scene. This has modified slightly since the advent of the internet, and even more so after smartphones and gay social networking applications like Grindr became commonplace. The immediate gratification potential has surged with technology and cyber-social media options.

Substance Use Facilitates an Alternate Reality

Some gay men use substances to deflect negative conclusions about their homosexual thoughts, feelings, and actions. Using substances or drinking can temporarily make it more comfortable for some to accept the reality of their homosexuality and other feelings of inadequacy and life stressors. Alcohol and other substances perpetuate delusions and reinforce a false self. Substance use can suppress the inhibitions that would otherwise contain a dismissive, "disposable people" mentality that some gay men can't help but display. For example, some gay men end up "hooking up" one time and then act like it never happened. Substance use and abuse makes casual, quasi-intimate, sexual liaisons more manageable and/or more intense and distinctive.

> *Alcohol and other substances perpetuate delusions and reinforce a false self.*

Substances provide a brief, deceptive sense of relief and escape from past traumas; this may include managing feelings like shame and distressing unwanted emotions.

12-Step Programs Offer Social and Emotional Support

Thinking and acting in alcoholic ways are a telltale sign of being blocked over time. If self-medicating is necessary to cope with life, it is likely that serious blocking is driving the behavior. 12-step programs, such as Alcoholics Anonymous (AA) and similar 12-step groups, are a common modality accessed when drugs, alcohol, addictions, and compulsive behaviors become unmanageable. 12-step programs are social and emotional support systems as well as a framework to follow for treatment and stability. The 12-step principles suggest that addicts are out of control but also need to take responsibility for their behaviors, choices, boundaries, and actions. If desired, LGBTQ+-centric 12-step meetings are offered in most cities.

Those struggling with addictions may find help in treatment programs, both inpatient and outpatient, 12-step meetings, groups, and individual counseling. Most recovery efforts will attempt to identify and unravel the underlying problems, issues, and triggers that substance use is a symptom of and promote healthier coping mechanisms.

Recovery Benefits

For addicts, the recovery process or the maintenance of sobriety involves removing the substance in an effort to deal with the underlying issues. Individual therapy is also part of recovery. Depending on the situation, a combination of therapy, psychiatry, inpatient, outpatient, 12-step, and various rehabilitation programs may be indicated.

The goal of recovery is to assist with efforts to unblock the frequently extensive history of what has been blocked and medicated with substances. Rather than using denial and substances to self-medicate, healthier coping mechanisms are encouraged. Some gay men struggling with alcoholic behaviors remain distressed because they have not unconditionally accepted their gay sexual orientation without the approval of others.

Gay men in recovery will benefit from overcoming their compensating ego and grandiose, distorted sense of self. Becoming sober and becoming unblocked are closely linked. Being familiar with what the M-Ranking variables are and how these superficial, idealized values specifically plague gay men is a crucial step toward empowerment and wellness.

> *Rather than using denial and substances to self-medicate, healthier coping mechanisms are encouraged.*

Sex, Sex, and More Sex

Visual marketing and promotional efforts within the GMC often cultivate a dynamic and environment that are highly reinforcing and provoking when it comes to prioritizing sex and sexualization as a social norm in the community. Sexual conquests can become a source of validation and affirmation, as well as a compulsive entity for many gay men, at least for a while in their adult lives.[68]

Gay men tend to be very sexually focused. Many are reacting to years of being blocked from normal, readily accessible, authentic same-sex experimentation; some feel more free and are making up for lost time. The blocking history in childhood specifically impacts sexuality and ultimately limits homosexual activity and experimentation; thus, it causes significant repression and potential for delayed sexual compulsivity into adulthood. The history of restriction intensifies the emphasis that adult gay men place on sex, sexualization, and sexual activity.

Hypersexualized displays by gay men are regularly seen on nonsexual/non-hookup applications, such as standard social media posts (including those that are not presumed to be primarily sexual, such as TikTok, Instagram, or similar sites), where some gay men amplify sexual innuendos of themselves. They sometimes portray themselves provocatively, with little insight or awareness that this is not a sexual hookup site, and that being persistently sexually suggestive everywhere lacks humility and deters from the point they're trying to make.

Gay men tend to be very sexually focused.

They may be pontificating and virtue signaling about how *all* gay men should act, reciting frustration about bad gay behavior in "our community," yet not realizing that this is also self-applicable. Seeking attention and validation through inappropriate hypersexualization is predictable behavior for some gay men; the attention-seeking dramatics are also histrionic, with more extreme versions actually diagnosed as histrionic personality disorder (HPD). These actions are another derivative after years of being blocked and following suit with the influence of the M-Ranking values and implications of the narcissistic spectrum.

PART V

Choice Information

CHAPTER 18

Choices and Boundaries

Sexual orientation is not chosen. No human being chooses the sexual orientation they are born with. We do not choose whether we are born as a homosexual (gay) or heterosexual (straight) person, nor do we choose whether we are born in the biologically based, genetic state that we are. There are specific choices connected to how we experience and identify ourselves, our families, our children, and our gay children, if applicable.

Some people continue to insist that gay men choose to be gay and that gay men can also choose to change their gayness, which is not possible. Achieving equality and normalization for LGBTQ+ people and for homosexuality, in general, is impeded by misconceptions like these.

Nobody Chooses to Be Gay or Straight

No one chooses their sexual orientation, including heterosexuals and homosexuals. It is preposterous to suggest that gay men would choose to be discriminated against and subject themselves to all the negative responses and challenging or threatening circumstances they are potentially exposed to for their entire lives.

A greater percentage of gay people live more openly and freely than in the past, and there is less repression and more tolerance. Increasing numbers of different people interact with gay men in some capacity. However, there are those who continue to maintain that gay men can alter their sexual orientation by making a different choice;

some judging, less tolerant people even proclaim that gay men could and *should* literally choose not to be the way they naturally are. These are ignorant presumptions that can be readily debunked by questioning millions of gay men; almost all of them will adamantly concur that they absolutely did not just choose to be gay.

Being Gay Is Not a Choice That Can Be Changed

Ignorance and intolerance of homosexuality will not make gay men straight. Most gay men who choose to stay closeted do so because they fear being shamed, being judged and "missing out" on a "normal" life. Many people in the United States don't care about the relationships or sexual activity of other adults. Unfortunately, there are plenty who do not accept homosexuality.

It would be beneficial to the GMC if more people would *choose* to be informed, aware, and tolerant. Increased awareness and tolerance about gay men directly elevates levels of respect, both individually and collectively in all communities.

As of June 2024, an estimated 8.1 billion people populate the earth.[69] A global survey in June 2023 estimates that about 9% of the population identify as "LGBTQ."[70] There may be 300–400 million gay men worldwide; even just half that number (about 2% of the world's population) amounts to several hundred million gay men worldwide. The actual number is likely higher than 2%, but this statistic cannot be precisely confirmed because it is contingent upon valid self-reporting.

CRITICAL THINKING CHOICE CHECKPOINT #17

Gay men should continue to educate less tolerant, less aware, straight-identifying people in their lives (and sometimes other less-aware gay men) to consider various critical thinking and analyses about gay men they've met.

Bullying and Discriminating Are Cruel, Punitive Choices

Making the choice to be intolerant or to discriminate, shame, or bully gay men is especially destructive; it is particularly outrageous behavior when spearheaded by a gay man's own family. Choosing to casually disregard the potential fragility of their own son is reprehensible on the part of family members, but it is quite common. It isn't the gay son's fault if their family acts in such an asinine manner.

Most rejecting families base their thinking on premeditated choices to maintain and promote a nonsupportive, anti-gay mentality. Intolerant family members need to accept the reality rather than resist being properly informed that sexual orientation is not a choice.

Gay Men Do Not Choose to Be Discriminated Against or Bullied

Gay men have no control over their innate sexual orientation other than to acknowledge and affirm it, lie about it, hide it, or minimize it. Some gay men choose not to openly acknowledge their gayness, and they may never do so. Young gay boys have little control over the external environment's disrespect and punitive, hateful response to gay boys and gay people. Gay men have been invalidated by an unhindered impact of homophobia for many years. In some cases, gay children have some choice as to how they respond to the external exposure and treatment from others, but this becomes mainly relative once they are adults or if they are lucky enough to have more supportive, well-informed parents during their childhood years.

A certain percentage of the population will remain critical of gay men, regardless of social pressure.

Anti-gay intolerance may persist because of those who choose to be or remain misinformed, intolerant, ignorant, and hateful. A certain percentage of the population will remain critical of gay men, regardless of social pressure.

Victim or Victor?

Nobody invites insensitive, anti-gay subjugation or chooses to be victimized. However, after this treatment happens and after they enter the adult GMC, gay men have a choice to leave victimhood.

Gay adulthood and the GMC pose other potential violations. Gay men also stand to be disrespected by other gay men. The choice to be or remain a victim is there regardless of the discrimination that gay men endure. The continuing improvement in social, political, and legal fronts is not always extensive. Gay male adults, like any other oppressed group, are ultimately responsible for improving their own situations.

The choice to be or remain a victim is there regardless of the discrimination that gay men endure.

CHAPTER 19

The Closet Conundrum: Stay in or Come Out?

A certain percentage of gay men choose to openly acknowledge and accept their sexuality, while others are more private or closeted. The exact number cannot be confirmed as some remain more private about their sexual orientation.

Some gay men choose to marry women, mostly in an attempt to be viewed and live as straight men (straight-normal). Making a choice to repress or avoid gayness is their option; however, it hinders the collective progression of gay affirmativism.

Gay men who choose to hide their sexuality or marry women contribute to a collective effect of limiting the mainstream world from exposure to a constructive, informed tolerance for gay men. The more men who stay closeted, the less familiar they are to the mainstream world, and the less normalization of LGBTQ+ people occurs.

Some gay men view closeted gay men as lacking character; there are other people who view *being gay* as lacking character and highly undesirable; this includes some self-loathing gay men, regardless of how revealing they are about their sexuality. Anxiety and fear incentivize some gay men to remain closeted. These concerns often relate to job security, finances, family threats, reputation, or losing an opportunity to experience what they think is a "normal" life.

Those who choose to be out are normalizing their gayness. Choosing to present authentically normalizes gayness and reinforces *internal satisfaction*.

CRITICAL THINKING CHOICE CHECKPOINT #18

Gay men have the option to collectively educate and validate gay-affirmative awareness by choosing to come out of the closet. Those who choose to remain closeted, repressed, and blocked accomplish the opposite of gay affirmation. They will *not* positively influence the image and concept of gay men and gay causes or reinforce protective laws and statutes. The choice to stay in the closet sends a negative message to some that being gay or openly gay and self-accepting are undesirable. Also, anyone can still be out of the closet and maintain a personal level of discretion.

Why Closeted Homosexuals Are Offensive to Gay Men

Most gay men were previously in the closet and may have led a different life in their past. Theoretically, most of those who have come out have some prior experience with the struggles of being closeted. Gay men who have come out of the closet may be put off by those who are in the closet despite the relatability to their own past.

CRITICAL THINKING CHOICE CHECKPOINT #19

Whether to openly acknowledge or "come out" as gay is an individual decision. However, the collective impact of those choosing to stay repressed, hidden, and closeted reinforces a negative association about being a gay man. A choice to remain closeted reinforces a belief that being gay is an undesirable shameful trait that should be hidden.

Choosing to Be in the Closet, Partially Out, or Widely, Openly Gay

Defining homosexual identity is an individual decision. Even with a long history of allegations, rumors, or gay indicators, traits, and behaviors, any gay man can respond to that reality in various ways. One decisive response is total denial of the gay sexual orientation, which may or may not be modified later. From here, a closeted gay man can choose various methods to maintain the closet for his protection; sometimes the closet maintenance may mean compromising someone else's life. This might involve active anti-gay projection on to openly gay men. Other closeted gay men may choose to marry a woman or "beard" to cover up the gayness.

THE COMING-OUT MATRIX

All gay men can ponder the pros and cons of their decision to come out, presenting more authentically. The final decision about if, when, where, or how to acknowledge gayness is an individual choice that includes timing and comfort levels.

Why Some Gay Men Stay Closeted

A percentage of gay men choose to stay closeted. Some of their reasons include:

- Less personally offensive
- Reputation
- Fear of losing relationships
- Fear of attacks
- Living a nontraditional life
- Being an oddity or in a stigmatized minority
- Religious ostracization
- Brainwashing and denial
- Exposure to intense shaming
- Weakness
- Fear of not "fitting in"
- Career/job implications

Staying closeted maintains a sense of safety and power. Ironically, some closeted gay men are not particularly masculine or even straight-acting, yet they still feel an entitled need to self-block and remain closeted as a viable option. The biggest obstacle for more obviously closeted gay men to stay comfortably closeted is that it is harder for them to hide their gayness.

Mixed Messages Sent by High-Profile Closeted Gay Men

Some gay men resent the negative message sent by closeted gay men. While it is anyone's prerogative to be closeted or "discreet," their choice sends a message that validates a negative belief that being gay is wrong, bad, and unacceptable. Some of the men who are not in the closet become offended and resent those privileged with celebrity status or a higher profile; it's as though they get a "pass" on dealing with potential and real strife and struggles that much of the GMC is faced with.

Higher-Profile Closeted Gay Men in Positions of Power and Influence

Celebrities and higher-profile people can draw the public's attention. Someone's sexual orientation may be none of the public's business, but people are curious and like to gossip; they can't help but observe what is exposed, especially with the influence of technology and social media.

It is not uncommon to find men in power positions or having some type of influence who are also gay and closeted. This may include people of authority in business management, CEOs, entrepreneurs, and those in political positions or serving as religious leaders, for example. Less-stable closeted homosexuals tend to be self-loathing, which creates a chronic state of internal conflict. Some closeted homosexuals are well-versed in displacing their emotions onto other gay men to reduce the impact of their own rage and self-loathing (this is also indicative of some Cluster B personality disorder traits—see Part IV).

A comfortable level of self-acceptance among gay men is somewhat undermined by those who remain closeted. Despite their reasons for continuing to live a lie or have a "beard" for their career, projecting and modeling closeted behavior hinder a normalization of gayness. When they lie and deny their gayness, it becomes more challenging for them to ever admit the truth. More authentic, normalized portrayal of gayness is compromised and blocked.

For celebrities, politicians, religious leaders, and other high-profile people, sneakiness and distorted projections may be highly publicized once exposed. Because of technology and social media, and because they are in the entertainment business, politics, or other conspicuous positions, falsehoods are harder to retract if the truth comes out.

Some are well-known as gay to many; however, many higher-profile gay men will never acknowledge or be truthful about their sexuality, even with the impact of technology and social media.

> *For celebrities, politicians, religious leaders, and other high-profile people, sneakiness and distorted projections may be highly publicized once exposed.*

Despite the risks of being found out and identified, many higher-profile gay males will do their best to remain permanently hidden in the closet, and *that* is their *choice*.

COST-BENEFIT ANALYSIS OF STAYING IN THE CLOSET OR COMING OUT	
STAY IN THE CLOSET/BLOCKED	**COME OUT OF THE CLOSET**
LARGELY BLOCKED Living a less authentic life	**LESS BLOCKED/UNBLOCKED** Being authentically oneself
SAFER FROM IMMEDIATE, SURFACE CONSEQUENCES Less immediate negative judging	**LESS SAFE/MORE EXPOSURE** More risk for being judged and disliked for being (more openly) gay
DIFFERENT/LESS JOB RISK Less scrutiny	**RISK IMPACTING/LOSING JOB** Unknown employer response
PRESERVE FAMILY Living as if straight	**LESS TRADITIONAL STATUS** Will not marry a woman
AVOID SOCIAL STIGMA Superficially straight	**RISK MORE JUDGMENT** True gayness exposed
BE IN THE MAJORITY Most people are not gay	**BE IN THE MINORITY** Gay is not the majority
RELIGIOUS PRESERVATION Accepted for being (presumed) straight	**RISK RELIGIOUS REJECTION** Rigid/less tolerant of gay men
DISCOUNT GAY SELF Sends a devaluing message	**SELF-RESPECT and EFFICACY** More inner and outer validation
ACCOMMODATE EXTERNAL Take care of others' comfort	**ACCOMMODATE INTERNAL** Less people-pleasing effort
IMPACT LEVEL OF ANXIETY Crazy-making to hide gayness	**LESS IMPACT LEVEL OF ANXIETY** May still have anxiety about being oneself vs. being neurotic about having to hide
RESTRICTED DATING/LIFESTYLE Either have to present as "straight-acting" or be on the "down-low" and go through the motions of dating women	**LESS RESTRICTION** Can date men more openly

STAY IN THE CLOSET/BLOCKED	COME OUT OF THE CLOSET
COLLECTIVE ANTI-GAY IMPACT Sends negative message	COLLECTIVELY GAY-AFFIRMING IMPACT Coming out sends positive message
PERPETUATES SENSE OF SHAME Closeted due to shame	PERPETUATES SELF-WORTH Being out reflects true self
EMOTIONALLY DRAINING Hiding is wasted energy	ENERGY AND EFFORTS USED MORE CONSTRUCTIVELY Being out allows for energy to be spent on self-improvement and self-care

Summary: Closeted or Not, Is It Worth It?

Coming out and acknowledging one's gayness can be incredibly stressful, sometimes risky, and often traumatic, primarily because of negative reactions from parents, family, friends, and community. However, being inauthentic to this capacity by staying closeted is also stressful and emotionally draining. Individual gay men must make an independent decision on how to proceed with their lives and their innate sexual orientation. This isn't a new dilemma; gay men have been making these difficult existential decisions for years, with many opting to stay hidden.

Staying blocked and closeted has consequences. Some closeted gay men start and/or limit their coming-out process by claiming they are bisexual. They do this in an effort to reduce their fears, which likely stem from their presumption of experiencing a potentially more negative response if others learn that they are identifying as "fully" gay. Other times, they get caught or "outed" somehow. When the

> *Individual gay men must make an independent decision on how to proceed with their lives and their innate sexual orientation.*

truth or more truthfulness comes out, there can sometimes be an even more negative, damaging impact than that of an original disclosure. The longer a gay man denies his sexuality, the more established and further away from the truth it becomes. We all have choices. Unfortunately, sexual orientation is not one of them.

PART VI

Unlocking and Unblocking Solutions and Resolutions

CHAPTER 20

The Unblocking Factor (U-Factor): Maximizing Internal Satisfaction

What can be done about the challenging, sometimes confusing lives that gay boys and gay men are often exposed to and inducted into? The M-Ranking, which correlates with part of the dynamics in the GMC of Dimension #3, is just one example of a more superficial, socially reinforced value system that can lead to a predictable search for mostly unattainable, exclusive perfection. Conforming and adhering to this agenda will generally produce limited returns.

In contrast, the Unblocking Factor, or *U-Factor*, supports a personally systemic goal of achieving internal satisfaction; it is an empowering set of positive values and goals that can be utilized to mindfully manage and challenge blocking. The theme of the M-Ranking reinforces a hypervaluation of mostly unachievable, idealistic traits of non-gayness and masculinity levels; this includes other superficial values that can feel like an incessant need for achieving a level of perfection or external approval or both.

The U-Factor emphasizes a healthy version of internal versus external focus. The goal is to maximize inner contentment to achieve self-acceptance as opposed to seeking external approval, all while still maintaining humility versus narcissism.

> **COMPONENTS OF THE UNBLOCKING FACTOR (U-FACTOR)**
>
> Positive proactive values and goals that can challenge and manage blocking:
>
> #1 Internal Satisfaction vs. External Approval
>
> #2 Insightful and Informed to Achieve Self-Acceptance
>
> #3 Integrity and Humility vs. Insincerity and Shallowness
>
> #4 Independence and Individuality vs. Cloning and Conforming
>
> #5 Intimacy vs. Blocked Superficiality

Emphasis on the U-Factor Instead of the M-Ranking: Internal Satisfaction Versus External Approval

Achieving internal satisfaction and self-acceptance decreases the need for external approval; maximizing the U-Factor components is the antithesis of striving for the more superficial M-Ranking, which is mostly based on aesthetics and materialism. Unblocking requires a focus on self-acceptance that is not contingent on outside evaluation and approval-seeking and does not entertain being heavily scrutinized by other gay men.

Many gay men develop a distorted belief that someone else must validate and approve of them in order for them to be okay. The reality is that prioritizing internal satisfaction is not contingent upon superficial, aesthetically based, pervasive need for external approval.

Many gay boys are indoctrinated to believe and conclude that *appearing* a certain way and seeking external approval is a fundamental requirement. As they enter the GMC in Dimension #3, some presume they have learned how to be accepted and will be successful. They may perceive a message from the GMC collectively promoting and overvaluing masculine perfection, model looks, being "well-endowed," and having wealth, status, and power. The external approval-seeking is enticing, yet the implications and influence of the M-Ranking will not unblock or cultivate fundamental internal self-acceptance. Pursuing superficial, externally based qualities for self and others is often disappointing.

Idealizing masculine perfection creates a façade that also fosters a need for external approval. Most gay men seeking external approval eventually end up feeling a lack of both external and internal approval; they can heal themselves, self-affirm, and reclaim an authentic sense of self by deflecting pressure to conform to the M-Ranking. Those who do not deflect will continue to facilitate a false persona, pursuant to the M-Ranking that blocks them from their true selves in the first place.

> *Most gay men seeking external approval eventually end up feeling a lack of both external and internal approval.*

M-Ranking Temptations Lead to More Blocking

Exercising and being fit in an effort to be and feel most attractive is admittedly a desirable accomplishment. At one juncture in their lives, many gay men make diligent efforts to measure up to the M-Ranking model. It is tempting to want to feel included and approved of by embodying what seems like preferred values in the GMC; however, meticulously adhering to the M-Ranking philosophy is less self-validating and less unblocking. The temptation to conform to a strong M-Ranking can lead to more blocking. Gay men holistically evolve through internal satisfaction. Some will struggle to move beyond the less mature, shallower aspects of the M-Ranking.

The M-Ranking evaluation process exists in parts of the GMC dynamics, whether an individual supports it or not. The M-Ranking valuation is just one set of admired influential, behavioral, and social norms in the GMC; it may seem extremely universal as something that most all gay men may prioritize. However, it certainly is not a requirement, nor the only framework that is blindly followed by every gay man. With maturity comes greater enlightenment, awareness, and insight; hence, the M-Ranking valuation can lose its subjective grip if gay men choose to reject it.

New Ways of Thinking: Prioritize the U-Factor Over the M-Ranking

Authenticity is devalued when gay men overemphasize male perfection, including qualities like masculinity, manhood, model looks, materialism, and mainstream appeal. Perhaps for some, pursuing the ideal of masculine and visual perfection celebrates the idea of acquiring or associating with a more neutral or less obviously gay image.

Those seeking to comply with the M-Ranking can reframe their views to understand that compliance often creates a paradox. It is a distortion to think that having what some consider a higher M-Ranking creates genuine satisfaction when this value system is ultimately contingent upon the actions and approval of someone or something else.

Accommodating Others Is Not the Responsibility of Gay Men

A strong U-Factor affirms a sense of self-respect and self-acceptance without needing to people-please other gay men. The historical defense of blocking self and others is not necessary to entertain as an adult.

Self-acceptance is individually defined and increases internal satisfaction by strengthening self-worth and *self-efficacy*. "Self-efficacy reflects confidence in the ability to exert control over one's own motivation, behavior, and social environment."[71] The affirmation here is "I am doing it."

> **CRITICAL THINKING CHOICE CHECKPOINT #20**
>
> Be yourself as you define it. Choose to self-empower. Self-designation and self-efficacy (the ultimate belief in applying profound self-confidence by taking action) occurs after decreasing the need for approval from external sources, including family, friends, mainstream communities, and especially other gay men.

The U-Factor Is About Substance and Depth

Becoming more self-contained facilitates healing from years of damage caused by faulty thinking and unnecessary emotional and behavioral reactions; years of distorted thoughts are the result of indoctrination that defined "normal" as being straight-normal. The U-Factor variables—such as internal acceptance, insight and empathy, integrity, and intimacy development—are powerful entities of substance, whereas being forcefully straight-acting or straight-passing, wealthy, popular, and having youthful, model-like beauty are more of a storybook façade of perfection.

Benefits of Internal Satisfaction

Feigning being straight perpetuates people-pleasing and blocks authenticity. Internal acceptance begins with introspective thinking and self-reflection; gay men can consider what will or won't transpire from garnering idealized, external approval and acceptance.

Unblocking and becoming an evolved, empowered gay adult requires unlocking and reprogramming distorted thoughts. Developing internal satisfaction will minimize or extinguish the need for approval. Empowered gay men must make a choice to dismiss the impact of actual or potential external judgments by everyone, including other gay men.

CHAPTER 21

Insightful and Informed Versus Shallow, Detached, and Unaware

Insight refers to the capacity to construct a thorough comprehension of a concept or a person, including oneself. Adequate functional insight requires developing a deeper awareness of self and others. The American Psychological Association (APA) defines *insight* as "the clear and often sudden discernment of a solution to a problem by means that are not obvious and may never become so, even after one has tried hard to work out how one has arrived at the solution."[72]

Empathy refers to the ability to grasp a reasonable anticipation of what another person is feeling, as well as what and how that feeling influences their experience. The APA defines *empathy* as "understanding a person from their frame of reference rather than one's own, or vicariously experiencing that person's feelings, perceptions, and thoughts."[73]

Intuition or being intuitive implies a process of readily understanding something or someone else without a need for an explicit and detailed explanation. The APA defines *intuition* as "immediate insight or perception, as contrasted with conscious reasoning or reflection. Intuitions have been characterized alternatively as quasi-mystical experiences or as the products of instinct, feeling, minimal sense impressions, or unconscious forces."[74]

Boundaries describe a perceived limit of various capacities between two people or one person and other groups of people, or sometimes between groups of people. Boundaries may dictate behaviors, including what views and beliefs are maintained and what comments or actions are taken or not. Being mindful about boundaries means applying critical thinking to various decisions and having purpose and appropriate self-control. Healthier boundaries include the capacity to think of the impact one's actions will have on another or others, and the other way around. The APA defines a *boundary* as "a psychological demarcation that protects the integrity of an individual or group or that helps the person or group set realistic limits on participation in a relationship or activity."[75]

> *Healthier boundaries include the capacity to think of the impact one's actions will have on another or others, and the other way around.*

Developing keener insight means having adequate empathy and intuitiveness. An insightful person would be able to pause their thinking and wonder, "What is really going on here? What and where am I in relation to the rest of the world?"

Proper levels of insight about self and others facilitate an appropriate, thoughtful response to perceived boundaries; an individual can potentially recognize and implement some sense of boundaries. This may include boundaries that are personally set as well as acknowledging, respecting, and responding in a suitable manner to those perceived to be set forth by other people or groups.

Gay boys are subjected to boundary violations when they are blocked, redirected, and shamed with anti-gay conditioning; rather than continue this dysfunctional behavior, as adults, they have more opportunity to begin unblocking. Gay men need to learn to redirect various boundary violations by setting their own self-affirming boundaries.

Insight can be utilized to make decisions to stop unhealthy

exchanges with other people or groups of people. More common sense is created through insight, including development of reasonable expectations for yourself and others. Gay men can improve their self-worth and self-respect by setting healthier boundaries with all communities, gay or straight.

Inadequate insight is primarily caused by an underdeveloped sense of empathy as well as a deficient understanding of self and others. Some may jump to various value judgments (presumptuous stereotypes) about gay men but not fully determine anything of true substance. Conversely, some gay men boast about a self-proclaimed sense of depth, tolerance, and humanism, but they may not realize that they can be superficial and judgmental to others, including other gay men.

> Inadequate insight is primarily caused by an underdeveloped sense of empathy as well as a deficient understanding of self and others.

Some gay men make the mistake of relying on the approval of others, whether that approval is from straight people or other gay men. Placing a premium on acceptance and approval does not equate to feeling adequate. Strictly obtaining external approval is not relative to being an insightful, more informed gay man.

Narcissism in SJW Clothing Is Not Insight

Social media platforms have become an epicenter where limited insight fuels judging and blocking others and sometimes fosters obnoxious displays. Some gay men position themselves as "social justice warriors" (SJW) by posting videos and other content on various sites, such as TikTok, Facebook, Instagram, or X (formerly Twitter). One depiction frequently seen shows an attractive, attention-seeking, frequently shirtless gay man who is also apparently trying to send a meaningful message. A clichéd, recycled version consists of preaching a message, such as "We need to be nicer to one another in our community." The reality is that *you* need to be nicer, and while you're being so nice, consider being less sexualized and gratification-seeking.

Some misinformed gay men will pontificate about controversial subjects or offer entitled complaints about other gay men. Many don't realize they are promoting and sexualizing their own image for attention and validation; most of these intentions are ultimately for narcissistic self-gratification. Is posting sexually provocative content a constructive way to encourage humanitarianism? These are not examples of favorably advocating on behalf of other groups or for other gay men; to their chagrin, these depictions certainly do *not* support an effort to "be nicer" to one another.

GAY MEN DEFINING AND DEVELOPING INSIGHT

» **Focus on positive social etiquette with other gay men.** Know how to kindly and respectfully approach and engage gay men in person, online, and through social networking applications.

» **Learn from past experiences.** Make a reasonable effort to avoid repeating poor choices and behaviors and learn from mistakes.

» **Learn that other people don't define you.** This includes other gay men and biased, judgmental family members.

» **Overcome adversity and subjugation** from all sources, including bad feelings related to gay men or family.

» **Develop and be mindful of empathy** and more accurately anticipate other people's needs, including those of other gay men.

» **Be clear about what your needs are as well as the needs of someone else,** not yours or theirs exclusively.

> » **Use critical thinking to manage manipulation and sensationalism** in social media, various news outlets, and other information sources and venues. This includes not automatically accepting or believing everything, particularly identity politics. Think it through; does this really make sense to you? *Could you be wrong?*
>
> » **Understand yourself and those around you,** including other gay men. Know that everyone has a story and some historical reason for their story.
>
> » **Admit and accept that most humans are judgmental,** which can mean some discriminatory tendencies; deflect the notion that only gay men deal with being judged and discriminated against. Be aware of your own value judgments of others.
>
> » **Develop boundaries with improved awareness** and implementation instead of being codependent and arrogant.
>
> » **Accept your imperfections as well as those of others.** Not everyone, including you, likes or approves of everyone else.
>
> » **Appreciate more meaningful attraction** instead of superficial values and qualities; embrace the qualities found in the U-Factor.

Improving one's understanding and empathy through enhanced insight is similar to changing other aspects of thinking, such as working toward being less critical and rigid. An individual person can choose to be more empathetic by becoming more curious and inquisitive about other people and other things rather than being self-centered and stubborn. Develop a deeper sense of self; become more open-minded and less judgmental of others.

CHAPTER 22

Integrity and Humility: Independence and Individuality

Integrity is knowing right from wrong and upholding boundaries, empathy, and the unconditional value of other people. An individual with integrity will develop and follow some sense of personal ethics and morals. Integrity is about fostering a higher level of intellectual contemplation, including an individual's version of being thoughtful, honest, and reasonably logical. Adequate integrity includes maintaining an accurate acceptance of reality. The APA defines *integrity* as "the quality of moral consistency, honesty, and truthfulness with oneself and others."[76]

A person with integrity is likely to also have a sense of humility based on life lessons that favor being humble rather than egotistical; humility is the antithesis of arrogance and self-righteous entitlement.

For gay men, integrity may mean full acknowledgment of their sexuality and identity rather than some other vague reference or avoidant excuse. This pertains to gay men who insist their gayness is just a small part of them, or those who proudly self-identify as straight-acting or, in some cases, "bi-curious" in an effort to downplay their gayness. This posturing lacks humility and integrity, and is often based on ego, insincerity, people-pleasing, or elitism. Other ego-driven gay men will idolize and chase after heterosexual, unavailable men. Those seeking inappropriate mates may be struggling to establish solid integrity, self-worth, and self-respect. Overly conforming to the M-Ranking values will generally not include much integrity.

As they enter the GMC, rather than foster a sense of integrity, some gay men adopt a sense of aloof nastiness. Similar to high school dynamics, some feel coerced into engaging in disingenuous behaviors; they may be prone to creating inauthentic personas. This sometimes includes being in the closet or deflecting scrutiny about their true self. Repressing sexual identity in favor of presenting a false persona is challenging to a healthy level of integrity.

Blocking from the Past Can Lead to a Lack of Integrity

Humility cannot be readily achieved when integrity is compromised, especially for children. It is challenging for gay boys to easily and quickly deflect pressure to repress and block their gayness. As they mature into adulthood, gay men must overcome this violation in order to establish healthy integrity.

During childhood, many gay boys essentially lose a natural opportunity and right to develop fundamental self-respect. In order to self-protect and survive these years, many were manipulated and pressured to be straight-normal, which compromised their integrity.

After years of being blocked and repressed, some gay men may still feel coerced into "skirting around" their authenticity. Feeling pressured to minimize, deny, or lie about who you are does not foster integrity. Individual gay men can challenge incorrectly learned, demeaning, anti-gay conclusions.

CRITICAL THINKING CHOICE CHECKPOINT #21

Cultivating integrity may require a premeditated, diligent, and mindful effort. Unblocking or the U-Factor means that individuals are accepting of their true authentic selves without people-pleasing. Authentic self-acceptance is an affirmative act of self-respect.

There are multiple consequences of being blocked from adequate integrity development in childhood. Some gay men play mind games with other gay men that may involve lying, hiding, faking, and avoiding. Perhaps there is a link between growing up as a well-acted gay boy trying to be something else and later pursuing an acting career in the entertainment industry. While there is a positive influence and history of gayness in acting, gay men who creatively act as professional actors and entertainers may perceive less pressure to conform, leaving them to be and feel freer in their "characters." The only requirement here is to become a believable version of the character they are playing for the performance they are in.

Prioritizing excessive conformity supports an unhealthy pattern of people-pleasing and approval-seeking. Less secure gay men who lack integrity are sometimes nasty and disrespectful to other gay men. Being a social-climbing opportunist does not promote humility.

Reintroducing Integrity After a History of Growing Up with Less or No Control

Most integrity-blocking childhood experiences for gay boys were out of their control. Often, integrity must be reintroduced to gay men as adults. Gay men are invited to be more mindful and cognizant in order to develop a sense of integrity, including understanding what integrity means to them.

Integrity Development Includes a Sense of Independence and Individuality

Gay men can choose to conform to the scrutiny of the M-Ranking or relearn and reclaim how to be themselves. They may have to restore their own identity rather than perpetually conforming to gay norms or the M-Ranking values.

Gay men must determine what their sense of individuality will become, which may also still include being a part of some gay male community.

> ## QUALITIES OF INTEGRITY AND HUMILITY
>
> Consider these ways to reintroduce integrity:
>
> » **Authentic and honest.** Be tactful and up-front without being phony.
> » **Humility.** Be modest and confident rather than egotistical or arrogant.
> » **Acceptance of self and others.** Understand human nature and imperfections. Recognize that some people may always dislike other people or situations, including gay men, which is not your problem.
> » **Reasonable expectations of self and others.** De-emphasize approval-seeking.
> » **Reasonable levels of respect for self and others** including balance and self-awareness.
> » **Value depth rather than superficiality.** Be interesting, unique, modest, and relatable.
> » **Available for interpersonal intimacy.** Be willing to share various degrees of personal reality.

Finding an Independent, Individual Identity After Coming Out Isn't Automatic

As they prepare to transition to early adulthood, some gay men may have high hopes that they will be freer to establish personal independence. One would hope the blocking would have mostly concluded or greatly reduced at this point. Most gay men who come out and are open realize that adequate clarity is not a guarantee; they will still need to work through further unblocking to figure out their individuality as a gay man in the GMC. This doesn't mean they have to be like every single other gay male, nor does it mean they have to become an extraordinary anomaly, or be especially involved in any particular scene.

The M-Ranking variables promoting an idealized male perfection can be a tempting framework to emulate. In contrast, by embracing maturity, experience, and common sense, gay men can comprehend other options from which to self-define. More evolved, independent gay men determine a self-identity that is less heavily influenced by other people, including the scrutiny from other gay men.

Balancing Individuality with Community

Coming out and connecting with some version of a gay male community is enticing but can be clouded by a paradoxical effort by many to not conform to what they were before they came out: a closeted gay kid trying to be straight. Many gay men will benefit from identifying as individuals while also connecting to a GMC. It is possible to be independent and an individual, and also maintain some connection, joining with other gay men if desired.

Being independent but still connected means being able to maintain personal integrity despite any peer pressure stemming from male perfectionistic ideals in the GMC. This process limits becoming overly conforming to various prototypes in the GMC. Gay men with healthier levels of humility and integrity are less likely to adopt a narcissistic, ego-driven value system.

Many gay men will benefit from identifying as individuals while also connecting to a GMC.

Distinguishing individuality may include a period of temporary conformity to learn how to be an individual and authentic in a community with other gay men. Some of the apparent role models are other gay men who are not necessarily the most individually solid.

There is a dialectic of trying to conform to some ideal versus mitigating efforts to not feel the need to rigidly conform to other norms in or out of the gay male community.

CHAPTER 23

Intimacy

The American Psychological Association defines *intimacy* as "characterizing close, familiar and usually affectionate or loving personal relationships, and requires parties to have a detailed knowledge or deep understanding of each other."[77] When considering interpersonal relationships, intimacy is a complex concept; it refers to a type of closeness generated by sharing one's personal reality. Intimacy is cultivated through various types of meaningful connections.

Different degrees of intimacy are established in numerous forms; this may include intimacy between close friends, significant others, family, acquaintances, neighbors, coworkers, peers, sexual liaisons or hookups, and more.

Pressuring gay boys to be straight-normal compromises their potential for organic intimacy development. Because of being shut off or shut down for self-protection, gay boys tend to struggle through childhood and into adulthood with comfortably allowing emotional intimacy to happen. These adversities can inhibit more meaningful connections beyond casual sexual encounters. True intimacy for gay boys would mean fully understanding, revealing, and sharing their true selves, while engaging in a more authentic and intimate interaction rather than remaining guarded; even age-appropriate natural intimacy development is restricted for most gay boys because many are being blocked by their parents and society.

Being present and sharing your authentic reality is less about being ultra-discreet or whether or to what extent you engage in the "gay social scene," or how straight-acting or -passing you are. Some gay men insist that sexuality and being gay is only a minor part of their character and overall identity. Contrary to this assertion, the fundamentals for the development of true selves are contained *within* the gay self.

Without parental coercion or external environmental interference, a more authentic and natural evolution of behaviors, interests, and expression of feelings and beliefs would be revealed. Because of this well-established blocking process, fundamental intimacy development continues to be a challenge for many gay boys and adult gay men.

Intimacy Development May Be Different for Gay Men

In general, many males, regardless of sexual orientation, are prone to some challenges in achieving healthy, emotionally intimate relationships. Society tends to groom men to be more emotionally stoic. Intimacy development for most heterosexual children is expanded during adolescence; however, many gay adolescents feel restrained and uncomfortable engaging in this manner.

Some gay men may feel safer and less challenged keeping their sexual and emotional intimacy separate. This is sometimes deliberately arranged as a limited casual sexual encounter, such as "friends with benefits," or a hookup. It is more challenging for some gay men to fully integrate both emotional and physical/social intimacy together. Some gay male relationships are notoriously more flexible and categorized as "open." Some maximize companionship and intimacy, which can function fairly well, even if sexual or physical intimacy is lacking; for some gay men, the open relationship or "ethical non-monogamy" status allows for more freedom to meet part of the intimacy needs that are deficient in the main relationship. Others have a level of physical

> *Some gay men may feel safer and less challenged keeping their sexual and emotional intimacy separate.*

and sexual intimacy without much if any emotional connection. They may feel forced to keep different types of intimacy separate; this may involve a gay man marrying a woman yet engaging in semi-regular gay sexual encounters with other men outside the traditional heterosexual marriage.

Intimacy Takes a Hit from a History of Homophobia, Hate, and Distrust

Gay boys compartmentalize or shut off and block out parts of themselves. They feel pressured to misrepresent themselves for self-protection. By adulthood, many become avoidant and guarded; they fear being punished and shamed again for being their true (gay) selves, which sometimes includes being openly intimate and freely trusting other gay men. Fear and anxiety may continue into adulthood/Dimension #3, including, during, and long after the coming-out process. Many are challenged to be comfortable achieving functional, intimate, committed, monogamous gay male relationships.

Men Seeking Men ("MSM") and Blurry Boundaries

Incorporating and merging both emotional and physical/sexual intimacy have proved more challenging for some gay men. Most gay boys are subjected to repression and restriction even if they made some effort to be more openly gay and come out of the closet. Many gay teens fall behind their straight peers in experiencing healthy intimacy. This process has more opportunities to develop when gay men are able to explore coming out as an adult, which may be delayed for many years.

Same-sex relationships can pose alternate social norms and dynamics, such as defining the difference between friends and lovers or friends with benefits. This sometimes manifests when gay men deal with a system of complex blocking dynamics while in pursuit of other compromised gay men who are in a similar predicament. The reality is that some may not want intimacy or are unable to connect emotional intimacy with physical/sexual intimacy. In some regard, this level of comfort "has" to be personally acceptable, if that is the extent of their emotional capability.

Value Judging and Seeking Perfection Inevitably Block Intimacy

The restrictive and superficial approach of the M-Ranking criteria can systemically limit intimacy. Adhering to the more superficial M-Ranking System blocks intimacy by demanding that stringent criteria must be met. Gay men seeking this type of perfection rule out and eliminate those they deem less desirable.

Mental Health and Emotional Immaturity Impact Intimacy

Developing healthy intimacy comes from a mastery of being authentic, vulnerable, and trusting others. Much of the dating/relationship experience gay men had as children was either underdeveloped or inauthentic. The frequency of abnormal intimacy development in gay boys is often a result of pandering to external pressures to "play the game" as if they were straight. This may sometimes result in frantic efforts to restrict close relationships as a way to hide their shameful gay secret.

Gay men are more likely to have a limited and complicated history of comfortably embracing and accepting their sexual identity. Other times, some of the intimate relationships they do have, including those with friends, are contrived or dysfunctional, makeshift opportunities.

By adulthood, some have a deficient or deluded sense of what intimacy means, leaving them ill-prepared to be involved in intimate relationships. For example, some blocked gay adolescents may feel obligated to hide their gayness by dating female peers; they may have "girl*friends*" or date girls but adhere to sexual restrictions and aversions, making up various excuses because they are not sexually attracted to females. Through the process, many are fully cognizant that they are acting insincerely; this creates mixed emotions of fear, a false sense of comfort, a conflicted yearning for what they really want, and resentment or rage for feeling pressure to hide and reinvent their inauthentic persona. Like anyone, gay boys have a common need to be themselves and be intimate in a way that reflects who they are *instead of who they feel someone else expects them to be.*

Like anyone, gay boys have a common need to be themselves and be intimate in a way that reflects who they are instead of who they feel someone else expects them to be.

Unlike many others, gay boys frequently do *not* get that seemingly simple, basic, merited need met. Some gay men will continue their journey to more accurately comprehend and create intimate relationships. Others are chronically conflicted or perplexed, maintaining a distorted interpretation of themselves and what a functional intimate relationship consists of. Gay men have to accept that some of the men they establish connections with may also have an inadequate capacity for healthy intimacy. In more severe cases, this includes the presence of serious mental health issues, like personality disorders.

Enhancing Intimacy

Before 2015, legal restrictions, especially the denial of same-sex marriage rights, deterred open gayness and made it more challenging for gay men to marry and build families. Combined with the pervasive dismissive and unequal treatment by large parts of society, the development of intimacy for gay men was negatively affected.

Gay men need to learn more about intimacy as they evolve, which means they may define it differently. What some consider to be intimate may not be healthy or sustainable. Gay men exist with varied degrees of "outness," which correlates to how comfortable they are being romantic or sexual with another male.

"Intimacy Blocks" Undermine Healthy Relationships

Gay men must thoughtfully assess to what extent they have felt dishonored in their lives; for some, this includes violations that make them feel fearful to be present and intimate with other people, other men, and other gay men.

Various examples of intimacy blocks can be incited by the treatment and attitudes in childhood and into adulthood from parents and family (Dimension #1) and teachers, friends, mainstream straight society, and religious entities (Dimension #2). Sometimes, gay men in the GMC (Dimension #3) develop intimacy blocks as a function of their immaturity, previous damaged relationships, poor choices, ignorance, profound inexperience, or distorted thinking.

> Some gay men may get as far as entering into an intimate same-sex relationship, but one or both partners will remain stuck at this point.

Self-blocking may continue into gay adulthood and undermine healthy intimacy development. Some gay men may get as far as entering into an intimate same-sex relationship, but one or both partners will remain stuck at this point. Other gay men experience blocked intimacy when they feel unfulfilled; their lack of trust and inadequate honesty lead to resentment and infidelity. Intimacy is also inhibited by substance abuse or other compulsive behaviors, including sexual addictions.

Intimacy is blocked for gay men when they embrace the historical parental pressure they felt to stay closeted and comply with a more avoidant, indifferent, "don't ask, don't tell" expectation. A history or present experience of conditional acceptance by a gay man personally or by his family-like support system can inhibit natural intimacy development in adulthood.

ANALYZING THE POTENTIAL FOR DEVELOPING HEALTHY ROMANTIC INTIMACY

The questions below are a starting point for assessing parameters of intimacy.

- How do you and the other gay man define intimacy, in terms of "sharing your reality"?
- What is your interest in this person?
- How do you define what a relationship is?
- How does the connection and bond manifest itself?
- Is there more to this connection than sex? If not, is that okay?
- What are the common interests?
- Is there an emotional *and* intellectual connection? Do both potential partners need this?
- Is there adequate companionship?
- Do you have similar or compatible backgrounds, values, interests, sources of joy, and passion?
- Is there a sense of support and altruism?
- Is there a healthy sense of reciprocity and interdependency?
- What do *you* contribute to the intimacy?
- What are your needs? What are you really looking for?
- How well developed and mutually present are the other U-Factors, like internal satisfaction, insight, integrity, and independence?
- Are the aesthetically or financially based M-Ranking assessments eroding the relationship somehow?
- Can you finally accept yourself unconditionally?
- Are you ready and willing to be your genuine self, what changes need to be made?

Rethinking Intimacy, Dating, and the Need for a Boyfriend or Husband

Some gay men may confuse idealized intimacy with an actual pursuit of expedited validation; they want to revel in the illusion of creating the perfect connection. Despite a genuine desire, some gay men struggle to achieve healthy intimacy and internal satisfaction.

Some gay men believe they want a more intimate, storybook relationship. However, after further exploration, they realize that they may not really want to follow a more traditional, committed heterosexual model, which is fine for them. However, gay men who are clear that they genuinely do desire a more traditional and complete intimate relationship have to be willing to share their reality. This means they accept the related challenges and potential consequences if the GMC, their family, or mainstream straight society is judgmental or disapproving. Those who seek a more committed, intimate relationship have to sort through others who either don't or won't want the same thing; some are not realistic in their expectations, which contradict their stated intention of finding an intimate companion.

Nothing Is Better Than Something when Seeking Perfection: With Aging and Time, Some Gay Men Really May Wind Up with Nothing

By being overly picky or grandiose, some gay men collaterally support a philosophy that nothing is better than something that is less than their perfectionistic expectations. Eventually, some really do wind up being alone, unable to achieve the intimacy they think or hoped they wanted.

In general, 30-something gay men still have fairly decent dating options. It is my experience that there are many gay men who remain unattached in their late 30s and into their 40s. Some continue their quest to satisfy the M-Ranking perfection requirements. The GMC is youth-centric and judgmental of older gay men. Parts of the GMC impede the development of intimacy by dismissing and devaluing older gay men, even as early as when they approach their 40s and 50s.

For some aging gay men, intimacy options can become more limiting as the frustration compounds into later decades of continuing disappointment; they are commonly dismissed by gay men of all ages—younger, similarly aged, and older. This desperation is sometimes projected as a vicious cycle of zero returns. More evolved, older gay men who are seeking monogamous relationships will have to be strategic in their dating and socializing.

This does not imply that gay men should disregard their needs and desires or that they have to embrace or not embrace anything at all, including the M-Ranking influence per se. From a clinician's perspective, becoming more flexible and establishing reasonable expectations of self and others will positively influence overcoming marginal dating outcomes.

Many gay men insist that they want a loving, fun, happy, outwardly appealing "long-term" relationship with another handsome, fit, well-equipped, eligible, *masculine* man. However, some will also contend that they just can't seem to find this idealized combination; other gay men may not feel deserving or may not truly want or be willing to commit to what an intimate relationship entails and requires. Still, others claim they don't want to be in a committed intimate relationship; they feel fed up, restricted, or are resolved and report that they are content being single and unattached. Some opt to have a healthy platonic support system that also does not leave them feeling blocked.

Conclusion

There are increasing numbers of openly gay men, improved levels of awareness and tolerance, and impressive political and legal progress. However, many gay boys growing up today and in the future will continue to be blocked initially from freely developing as they naturally are. A smaller number of gay boys will be fortunate enough to be influenced by more astute, supportive parents. Otherwise (and even still), it will be up to the gay boys and gay men to choose and learn to intervene to unlock and unblock themselves as they see fit and when they are able to do so.

Blocking gay boys is tragically unfair and oppressive; blocking can continue into adolescence and sometimes early adulthood. The abnormal interference that gay boys and gay men contend with will not simply dissolve and go away. *You've Been Blocked* has presented many of the issues related to this reality and discussed various ways to respond and react to this process. It invites parents, young gay men, gay adults, and other allies to elevate their awareness and understanding. It is critical that gay men not personify a victim who depends on external responses to create internal satisfaction.

Many gay men need to relearn messages from their childhood that heavily reinforced the idea that they must obtain external approval to be accepted. *You've Been Blocked* has outlined the value in focusing on internal acceptance and self-validation, especially once gay men are of legal age and have more capacity to do so. With this philosophy comes accountability to also maintain realistic expectations of self and others.

Gay men have a different developmental history, which requires that they achieve a more thorough understanding of how they were blocked beginning in childhood. This includes exploring what experiences are like today and what the future may consist of.

Homosexual orientation is a complex reality that gay boys are confronted with at a young, impressionable stage of child development.

At a certain point in this process, gay boys become more aware of their homosexuality, regardless of whether it is openly addressed or discussed, which it often is not.

Gay men don't choose to be born this way; it's just the way it is. And yet, most gay boys are, by default, put through an unbelievably challenging childhood, just for openers. Despite some social and legal progress, many gay boys are bombarded with negative feedback that tells them they are fundamentally wrong. This is how gay boys and later gay men are blocked from being their true selves. Many gay boys don't like being unable to just be themselves; they hate it, and why wouldn't they despise this violating treatment?

So, in essence, we have a gay boy who commonly doesn't exactly know how to fully interpret his feelings at the time; he doesn't entirely understand what being gay means at early junctures, and may not be completely cognizant yet of his own blossoming homosexuality. Regardless, the gayness is there, despite what less informed, insensitive, or heterosexist people choose to dissuade or disregard. Gay boys can develop severe anger and resentment as they realize they went along with a reckless process of repression. Most gay boys can only do so much while they are young versus when they are of legal age.

In order to feel less plagued by a sense of outrage, gay men have to figure out what to make of these complexities. For some, this

> *At a certain point in this process, gay boys become more aware of their homosexuality, regardless of whether it is openly addressed or discussed, which it often is not.*

means letting go of multiple layers of shame, resentment, and anger because they were blocked, and perhaps unknowingly allowing the blocking to happen.

Some Gay Men Will Overcome the Blocking History Better Than Others

Some gay men will persistently continue the search for gay male perfection and the M-Ranking valuation. Some may continue struggling to obtain or personify the values supported by the M-Ranking. Others may feel incapable of getting beyond (their perception of) the impact and priority of the M-Ranking in the GMC. Some may feel deficient, judged, or alienated for not meeting the perceived standards stemming from the influence of those overly judgmental gay men who choose to devotedly follow and personify the M-Ranking.

Sadly, some gay men continue to struggle to figure things out, even into their later years; they may not sufficiently complete the recovery work from being blocked as gay boys or younger gay men. Others will learn over time with age and experience and more thoughtful insight. Some will be enlightened by books, therapy, recovery programs, or influenced by informed people and more evolved gay men. Maintaining a hopeful, positive attitude for progress and improvement in the lives of gay men and future gay men involves a thoughtful, ongoing, open discussion of what the reality is like for developing gay boys. After genuinely extinguishing or minimizing a need for external approval, you've been unblocked.

Endnotes

1 Jones, J. (2024, March 13). *LGBTQ+ identification in U.S. now at 7.6%*. Gallup. Retrieved March 15, 2024, from https://news.gallup.com/poll/611864/lgbtq-identification.aspx

2 Barker, M. (2014). *Heteronormativity*. In Teo, T. (Eds.), Encyclopedia of critical psychology. Springer. https://doi.org/10.1007/978-1-4614-5583-7_134

3 The Trevor Project (2022, April 7). New Poll: Majority of U.S. Adults Are Comfortable Having LGBTQ Children, Fewer than 1 in 3 Know Someone Who is Transgender. thetrevorproject.org. https://www.thetrevorproject.org/blog/new-poll-majority-of-u-s-adults-are-comfortable-having-lgbtq-children-fewer-than-1-in-3-know-someone-who-is-transgender/

4 Movement Advancement Project. (n.d.). *LGBTQ youth*. https://www.lgbtmap.org/policy-and-issue-analysis/LGBTQ-youth

5 Zou, C., & Andersen, J. P. (2015). Comparing the rates of early childhood victimization across sexual orientations: Heterosexual, lesbian, gay, bisexual, and mostly heterosexual. *PLOS ONE 10*(10), Article e0139198. https://doi.org/10.1371/journal.pone.0139198

6 Burton, N. (2023, July 3). *When homosexuality stopped being a mental disorder*. Psychology Today. https://www.psychologytoday.com/us/blog/hide-and-seek/ 201509/when-homosexuality-stopped-being-mental-disorder

7 Pew Research Center. (2013, June 13). *A survey of LGBT Americans: Chapter 2: Social acceptance*. Pew Research Center. https://www.pewresearch.org/social-trends/2013/06/13/chapter-2-social-acceptance/

8 Pendharkar, E. (2022, October 25). *What school is like for LGBTQ students, by the numbers*. Edweek. Retrieved April 28, 2024, from https://www.edweek.org/leadership/what-school-is-like-for-lgbtq-students-by-the-numbers/2022/10#

9 McCloud, S., PhD (2025, April 18). *Erik Erikson's Stages of Psychosocial Development*. Simply Psychology. https://www.simplypsychology.org/erik-erikson.html

10 American Psychological Association. (n.d.). *APA dictionary of psychology*. Retrieved April 17, 2024, from https://dictionary.apa.org/validation

11 American Psychological Association. (n.d.). *APA dictionary of psychology*. Retrieved April 17, 2024, from https://dictionary.apa.org/shame

12 Todd, M. (2018, February 8). *Self-loathing among gay people is nothing new. We're

overwhelmed by it. The Guardian. https://www.theguardian.com/comment isfree/2018/feb/08/self-loathing-gay-people-shame

13 Todd, M. (2018, February 8). *Self-loathing among gay people is nothing new. We're overwhelmed by it.* The Guardian. https://www.theguardian.com/commentisfree/2018/feb/08/self-loathing-gay-people-shame

14 Miller, B., & Morawitz, E. B. (2016). "Masculine guys only": The effects of femmephobic mobile dating application profiles on partner selection for men who have sex with men. *Computers in Human Behavior, 62*, 175–185. https://doi.org/10.1016/j.chb.2016.03.088

15 Kaiser, J. (2019, August 29). *Genetics may explain up to 25% of same-sex behavior, giant analysis reveals.* Science.org. https://www.science.org/content/article/genetics-may-explain-25-same-sex-behavior-giant-analysis-reveals

16 Davis, G. E., & Mehta, C. M. (2022). "We are okay to be ourselves": Understanding gay men's friendships with heterosexual and gay men. *Psychology of Men & Masculinities, 23*(2), 209–221. https://doi.org/10.1037/men0000381

17 Brito III, J., & MacGill, M. (2022, December 23). *What size is the average penis?* MedicalNewsToday.https://www.medicalnewstoday.com/articles/271647

18 Grov, C., Parsons, J. T., & Bimbi, D. S. (2010). The association between penis size and sexual health among men who have sex with men. *Archives of Sexual Behavior, 39*(3), 788–797. https://doi.org/10.1007/s10508-008-9439-5

19 Whitfield, T. H. F., Rendita, H. J., Grov, C., & Parsons, J. T. (2019). Viewing sexually explicit media and its association with mental health among gay and bisexual men across the U.S. *Archives of Sexual Behavior, 47*(4), 1163–1172. https://doi.org/10.1007/s10508-017-1045-y

20 Neves, S., & Hagan, E. (2021, June 7). *Gay men and body perfection.* Psychology Today. https://www.psychologytoday.com/us/blog/talking-sex-and-relationships/202106/gay-men-and-body-perfection

21 American Psychiatric Association. (2022). *Diagnostic and statistical manual of mental disorders* (5th ed., text rev.). https://www.mredscircleoftrust.com/storage/app/media/DSM%205%20TR.pdf

22 Pope Jr., H. G., Philips, K. A., & Olivardia, R. (2002, January 10). *The Adonis complex: How to identify, treat and prevent body obsession in men and boys.* Free Press.

23 Lang, N. (2016, February 2). *Fat shaming, toxic masculinity, and the gay male beauty myth.* Daily Beast. Retrieved April 13, 2017, from https://www.thedailybeast.com/fat-shaming-toxic-masculinity-and-the-gay-male-beauty-myth

24 Zane, Z. (2018, July 31). *Gay men over 45 are most likely to be single according to AARP Study.* Out.com. https://www.out.com/news-opinion/2018/7/31/gay-men-over-45-are-most-likely-be-single-according-aarp-study

25 Wight, R. G., LeBlanc, A. J., Meyer, I. H., & Harig, F. A. 2015, December. Internalized gay ageism, mattering, and depressive symptoms among midlife and older

gay-identified men. *Social Science & Medicine, (147),* 200–208. https://doi.org/10.1016/j.socscimed.2015.10.066

26 Toesland, F. (2021, August 11). *The LGBTQ generational wealth gap.* Washington Blade. https://www.washingtonblade.com/2021/08/11/the-lgbtq-generational-wealth-gap/

27 Cooper, S., Péloquin, T., Lachowsky, N. J., Salway, T., Oliffe, J. L., Klassen, B., Brennan, D. J., Houle, J., & Ferlatte, O. (2023). Conformity to masculinity norms and mental health outcomes among gay, bisexual, trans, two-spirit, and queer men and non-binary individuals. *American Journal of Men's Health, 17*(5). https://doi.org/10.1177/15579883231206618

28 Liptak, A. (2021, October 14). *Civil rights law protects gay and transgender workers, supreme court rules.* The New York Times. https://www.nytimes.com/2020/06/15/us/gay-transgender-workers-supreme-court.html

29 Gower, A. L., Rider, G. N., McMorris, B. J., & Eisenberg, M. E. (2018). Bullying victimization among LGBTQ youth: Current and future directions. *Current Sexual Health Reports, 10*(4), 246–254. https://doi.org/10.1007/s11930-018-0169-y

30 Gerrard, B., Morandini, J., & Dar-Nimrod, I. (2023, February). Gay and straight men prefer masculine-presenting gay men for a high-status role: Evidence from an ecologically valid experiment. *Sex Roles* 88, 119–129. https://doi.org/10.1007/s11199-022-01332-y

31 Gower, A. L., Rider, G. N., McMorris, B. J., & Eisenberg, M. E. (2018). Bullying victimization among LGBTQ youth: Current and future directions. *Current Sexual Health Reports, 10*(4), 246–254. https://doi.org/10.1007/s11930-018-0169-y

32 G. K., & Brito, J., PhD, LCSW (2021, September 7). *Teenage dream or teenage scream? Why LGBTQIA+ people experience 2 kinds of adolescence.* Healthline.

33 Sánchez, F. J., & Vilain, E. (2012). "Straight-acting gays": The relationship between masculine consciousness, anti-effeminacy, and negative gay identity. *Archives of Sexual Behavior, 41*(1), 111–119. https://doi.org/10.1007/s10508-012-9912-z

34 Ryding, S. (2021, March 3). *What is seroconversion?* News Medical Life Sciences. https://www.news-medical.net/health/What-is-Seroconversion.aspx

35 Wright, J. (2013). Only your calamity: The beginnings of activism by and for people with AIDS. *American Journal of Public Health, 103*(10), 1788–1798. https://doi.org/10.2105/AJPH.2013.301381

36 Odets, W. (2019). *Out of the shadows: Reimagining gay men's lives.* Farrar, Straus and Giroux.

37 Berg, R. C., & Ross, M. W. (2014). The second closet: A qualitative study of HIV stigma among seropositive gay men in a southern U.S. city. *International Journal of Sexual Health, 26*(3), 186–-199. https://doi.org/10.1080/19317611.2013.853720

38 Ayala, G., & Spieldenner, A. (2021). HIV is a story first written on the bodies of gay and bisexual men. *American Journal of Public Health, 111*(7), 1240–1242. https://doi.org/10.2105/AJPH.2021.306348

39 Land, Emily. (2018, March 6). *You told us: HIV stigma still exists*. San Francisco AIDS Foundation. https://www.sfaf.org/collections/beta/you-told-us-hiv-stigma-still-exists/

40 CDC (n.d.). *HIV among gay and bisexual men*. CDC Fact Sheet (pdf). https://www.cdc.gov/nchhstp/newsroom/docs/factsheets/cdc-msm-508.pdf

41 Morton, J. (2024, March 25). Reflecting on 30 years of Poz. *Poz*. https://www.poz.com/article/reflecting-30-years-poz

42 (2025, February 7). Using HIV Medication to Reduce Risk. Hiv.gov. https://www.hiv.gov/hiv-basics/hiv-prevention/using-hiv-medication-to-reduce-risk/pre-exposure-prophylaxis

43 Carstens, A. (2023, June). *PrEP failures (breakthrough infections)*. AIDS map. https://www.aidsmap.com/about-hiv/prep-failures-breakthrough-infections

44 Land, E. (2018, March 6). *You told us: HIV stigma still exists*. San Francisco AIDS Foundation. https://www.sfaf.org/collections/beta/you-told-us-hiv-stigma-still-exists/

45 Rubinstein, G. (2010). Narcissism and self-esteem among homosexual and heterosexual male students. *Journal of Sex and Marital Therapy, 36*(1), 24–34. https://psycnet.apa.org/doi/10.1080/00926230903375594

46 American Psychiatric Association. (2022). *Diagnostic and statistical manual of mental disorders* (5th ed., text rev.). https://www.mredscircleoftrust.com/storage/app/media/DSM%205%20TR.pdf

47 Psychology Today (n.d.). Cluster b. *Psychology Today*. https://www.psychologytoday.com/us/basics/cluster-b

48 Bolton, S. L., & Sareen, J. (2011). Sexual orientation and its relation to mental disorders and suicide attempts: Findings from a nationally representative sample. *Canadian Journal of Psychiatry, Revue canadienne de psychiatrie, 56*(1), 35–43. https://doi.org/10.1177/070674371105600107

49 Zhang, T., Chow, A., Wang, L., Dai, Y., & Xiao, Z. (2012). Role of childhood traumatic experience in personality disorders in China. *Comprehensive psychiatry, 53*(6), 829–836. https://doi.org/10.1016/j.comppsych.2011.10.004

50 American Psychiatric Association. (2022). *Diagnostic and statistical manual of mental disorders (5th ed., text rev.)*. American Psychiatric Association. https://www.mredscircleoftrust.com/storage/app/media/DSM%205%20TR.pdf

51 American Psychological Association (n.d.). *What causes personality disorders?* www.apa.org. https://www.apa.org/topics/personality-disorders/causes

52 American Psychological Association (n.d.). *What causes personality disorders?* www.apa.org. https://www.apa.org/topics/personality-disorders/causes

53 White, C. N., Conway, C. C., & Oltmanns, T. F. (2020). Stress and personality disorders. In K. L. Harkness & E. P. Hayden (Eds.), *The Oxford handbook of stress and mental health* (pp. 183–197). Oxford University Press. https://psycnet.apa.org/record/2020-06187-008

54 Bearak, M., & Cameron, D. (2016, June 16). Here are the 10 countries where homosexuality may be punished by death. *The Washington Post*. https://www.washingtonpost.com/news/worldviews/wp/2016/06/13/here-are-the-10-countries-where-homosexuality-may-be-punished-by-death-2/

55 Corliss, H. L., Rosario, M., Wypij, D., Wylie, S. A., Frazier, A. L., & Austin, S. B. (2010). Sexual orientation and drug use in a longitudinal cohort study of U.S. adolescents. *Addictive Behaviors*, *35*(5), 517–521. https://doi.org/10.1016/j.addbeh.2009.12.019

56 Corliss, H. L., Rosario, M., Wypij, D., Wylie, S. A., Frazier, A. L., & Austin, S. B. (2010). Sexual orientation and drug use in a longitudinal cohort study of U.S. adolescents. *Addictive Behaviors*, *35*(5), 517–521. https://doi.org/10.1016/j.addbeh.2009.12.019

57 Rubinstein G. (2010). Narcissism and self-esteem among homosexual and heterosexual male students. *Journal of Sex & Marital Therapy*, *36*(1), 24–34. https://doi.org/10.1080/00926230903375594

58 Flowers, P., & Rosario, K. B. (2001). "I was terrified of being different": Exploring gay men's accounts of growing-up in a heterosexist society. *Journal of Adolescence*, *24*(1), 51–65. https://doi.org/10.1006/jado.2000.0362

59 American Psychiatric Association. (2022). *Diagnostic and statistical manual of mental disorders* (5th ed., text rev.). American Psychiatric Association. https://doi.org/10.1176/appi.books.9780890425787

60 American Psychiatric Association. (2022). *Diagnostic and statistical manual of mental disorders* (5th ed., text rev.). American Psychiatric Association. https://doi.org/10.1176/appi.books.9780890425787

61 White, C. N., Conway, C. C., & Oltmanns, T. F. (2020). Stress and personality disorders. In K. L. Harkness & E. P. Hayden (Eds.), *The Oxford handbook of stress and mental health* (pp. 183–197). Oxford University Press. https://psycnet.apa.org/record/2020-06187-008

62 McLeod, S., PhD (2023, July 10). *Freud's theory of personality: id, ego, and superego*. Simply Psychology. https://www.simplypsychology.org/psyche.html

63 American Psychological Association. (n.d.). Defense mechanism. *APA dictionary of psychology*. Retrieved January 23, 2024, from https://dictionary.apa.org/defense-mechanism

64 Cochran, S. D., Grella, C. E., & Mays, V. M. (2012). Do substance use norms and perceived drug availability mediate sexual orientation differences in patterns of substance use? Results from the California Quality of Life Survey II. *Journal of Studies on Alcohol and Drugs*, *73*(4), 675–685. https://doi.org/10.15288/jsad.2012.73.675

65 Hunt, J. (2012, March 9). *Why the gay and transgender population experiences higher rates of substance use*. American Progress. https://www.americanprogress.org/article/why-the-gay-and-transgender-population-experiences-higher-rates-of-substance-use/

66 U.S. Department of Health and Human Services. (2022, July). 2020 *national survey on drug use and health: Lesbian, gay, or bisexual (LGB) adults*. Substance Abuse and

Mental Health Services Administration. https://www.samhsa.gov/data/sites/default/files/reports/rpt37929/2020NSDUHLGBSlides072522.pdf

67 American Psychiatric Association. (2022). *Diagnostic and statistical manual of mental disorders* (5th ed., text rev.) 748–760. https://doi.org/10.1176/appi.books.9780890425787

68 Weiss, R. (2013). *Cruise control, understanding sex addiction in gay men* (2nd ed.). Gentle Path Press.

69 Worldometer. (n.d.). *Current world population*. Worldometer. Retrieved March 9, 2024, from https://www.worldometers.info/world-population/

70 Moreau, J. (2023, June 1). Global survey finds 9% of adults identify as LGBTQ. NBC News. https://www.nbcnews.com/nbc-out/out-news/global-survey-finds-9-adults-identify-lgbtq-rcna87288

71 American Psychological Association. (n.d.). *Teaching tip sheet: Self-efficacy*. American Psychological Association (APA). Retrieved January 20, 2024, from https://www.apa.org/pi/aids/resources/education/self-efficacy

72 American Psychological Association. (n.d.). Insight. *APA dictionary of psychology*. Retrieved April 17, 2024, from https://dictionary.apa.org/insight.

73 American Psychological Association. (n.d.). Empathy. *APA dictionary of psychology*. Retrieved April 17, 2024, from https://dictionary.apa.org/empathy

74 American Psychological Association. (n.d.). Intuition. *APA dictionary of psychology*. Retrieved April 17, 2024, from https://dictionary.apa.org/intuition

75 American Psychological Association. (n.d.). Boundary. *APA dictionary of psychology*. Retrieved April 17, 2024, from https://dictionary.apa.org/boundary

76 American Psychological Association. (n.d.). Integrity. *APA dictionary of psychology*. Retrieved April 17, 2024, from https://dictionary.apa.org/integrity

77 American Psychological Association. (n.d.). Intimacy. *APA dictionary of psychology*. Retrieved April 17, 2024, from https://dictionary.apa.org/intimacy

Index

Text boxes throughout the book are indicated by *italic* locators.

A
abuse/trauma. *see also* substance abuse
   blocking as, 10
   childhood, 4, 13, 15–16, 29, *48*, 118, 126–127
   hetero-normal and, 96
   narcissistic spectrum and, 118–124, 126–127
acceptance
   adequacy and, 177
   aging, of, 78
   alcohol and, 149
   anxiety and, 125
   bullying/mobbing and, 127
   closet, and the, 163
   coming out and, *160*
   identity and, 21, 124, 130
   insight and, 177
   intimacy and, 192
   M-Ranking System and, 52–53, 77, 84
   self, of, *48*, 65–66, 95
   U-Factor (unblocking factor) and, 169–173, *182*, *184*
   validation/invalidation and, 30
accommodation, 4, 52–53, 140, 172
acting-out, 13, 31, 32
adolescence
   alcohol and, 129
   authenticity and, 23, 26
   boys, and gay, 19–23
   bullying/mobbing and, 99
   conformity and, 84–85
   heteronormativity and, 27–28
   intimacy and, 96, 188, 190

   mental health and, 136
   narcissistic spectrum and, 116, 117–118
   validation-neutrality and, 29–30
aging, 80, 194–195
AIDS Project, 105
AIDS/HIV. *see* HIV/AIDS
alcohol. *see* substance abuse
alcohol, GMC and, 145–152, *147*
Alcoholics Anonymous, 150
American Psychiatric Association, 15
American Psychological Association (APA), 25, 118, 142, 175–176, 187, 192
anti-gay bias, 44, 66, 143, 157
antisocial personality disorder (APD), *119*, 120–121, *122*, 139
anxiety
   alcohol and, *147*
   closet, and the, 159, *164*
   HIV/AIDS and, 103–104, 109
   mental chatter and, *23*
   narcissistic spectrum and, 116, 125–126, 136
   shame and, *35*
APA (American Psychological Association), 25, 118, 142, 175–176, 187, 192
APD (antisocial personality disorder), *119*, 120–121, *122*, 139
appeal, mainstream (M-Ranking #5), 50, 83–86
approval
   external, 41–42, 169–173, 177, 197
   gay male community (GMC) (Dimension #3) and, 52–53

seeking of, 84, 124, 140, 183–184
atypical challenges, 12–13
authenticity
    adolescence and, 23, 26
    closet, and the, 159, *161*, 163, 165
    denial and, 137
    gay male community (GMC) (Dimension #3) and, 52
    integrity and, 182
    intimacy and, 84, 187–188, 190–191
    masculinity (M-Ranking #1) and, 58
    M-Ranking System and, 51–52
    narcissistic spectrum and, 122, 126
    U-Factor (unblocking factor) and, 172
azidothymidine (AZT), *107–108*

B

behavior, alcoholic, 145–152
bias, anti-gay, 44, 66, 143, 157
bisexuality, 125, 165
blocking defined, 1
borderline personality disorder (BPD), *119*, 120–121, *122*, 135
borderlining, *122*, 144
boundaries, 176, 189–190
    shame and, 176
boys, gay
    adolescence and, 19–23
    atypical challenges for, 12–13
    boundaries and, 176
    childhood development of, 2
    closet, and the, 23
    compensation and, 140
    defense mechanisms and, 139
    discrimination and, 157
    disorders, and identity, 135
    exploration, and sexual, 21–22
    future, and the, 197–198
    heteronomativity and, 9–10
    identity and, 1, 133, 135
    integrity and, 182–183
    intimacy and, 187–188, 189, 190–191
    masculinity (M-Ranking #1) and, 56
    narcissistic spectrum and, 122, 126–129
    reaction formation and, 143
    repression and, 22–23
    school, and primary, 16–18
    self-repression and, 3, 11
    sexual identity/orientation and, 136, 198
    U-Factor (unblocking factor) and, 170–171
    validation and, 26
BPD (borderline personality disorder), *119*, 120–121, *122*, 135
bullying/mobbing, 99, 127–128, 157–158

C

celebrities, closeted, 162–163
choice, gayness as, 155–158
Civil Rights Act (1964), 89
climbing, social, 41, 42, 52, 53, 84–86, 144, 183
closet, the
    analysis of, cost-benefit, *164–165*
    anxiety and, 159, *164*
    authenticity and the, 159, *161*, 163, 165
    boys and gay, 23, 30, 33
    celebrities and, 162–163
    gay male community (GMC) (Dimension #3) and, 43
    high-profile gay men and, 162–163
    integrity and, 181
    internalized homophobia and, 55
    intimacy and, 192
    narcissistic spectrum and, 125
    reaction formation and, 142–143
    shame and, 165
Cluster B personality disorders, 118–131, *119*, 120–121, *122*, 148, 163
codependency, 12, 129, 140, *147*, 179
coming out. *see also* closet, the
    boys and gay, 22
    closet and the, *161*, *164–165*, 165
    identity and, 134, 184–185
    intimacy and, 189
    masculinity (M-Ranking #1) and, 49
    M-Ranking System and, *48*
    upgrading and, 42
coming out matrix, *161*
community
    gay male (GMC) (Dimension #3), 39–45

mainstream (M-Ranking #5), 83–86
male perfection in (M-Ranking #3),
    48–54
manhood (M-Ranking #2) and, 63–67
masculinity (M-Ranking #1) and, 55–61
money/wealth (M-Ranking #4) and,
    79–81
physical perfection (M-Ranking #3)
    and, 69–78
compartmentalization, *122*, 138–139, 189
compensation, 17, 50, 74, 139, 140, 147, 151
compulsions, 129, 145–146, 150–152, 192
conformity, 12, 51, 83–86, 169, 171, 181,
    183, 185
confusion, identity. *see under* identity
confusion, role, 20–21
cost-benefit analysis of the closet,
    164–165
critical thinking choices
    blocking in the GMC (checkpoint #6),
        45
    closet, the (checkpoints #18-19), 160
    confusion, role (checkpoint #3), 20
    explained (checkpoint #1), 5
    hetero-normal and the (checkpoint
        #10), 85
    hetero-normal and the GMC
        (checkpoints #8, 14), 56, 98
    integrity (checkpoint #21), 182
    M-Ranking System in the GMC
        (checkpoint #7), 52
    narcissistic spectrum (checkpoint
        #16), 131
    orientation, sexual (checkpoint #17),
        156
    penis size (checkpoint #9), 65
    privilege, heterosexual male
        (checkpoint #11-13, 15), 89–90,
        92, 97, 101
    relationships (checkpoint #5), 41
    self-efficacy (checkpoint #20), 173
    society (checkpoint #2), 17
    validation (checkpoint #4), 27

D
defense mechanisms, 137–144
delusions, 144, 149–150

denial, 137–138, 142, 151, 161, *165*, 166
detachment, 131
development. *see also* identity; sexual
    identity/orientation
    arrested, 13, 116, 135
    identity, 10–11, 13, 125, 133, 135–136
    sexual, 10–11
*Diagnostic and Statistical Manual of
    Mental Disorders* (DSM), 15, 117–118,
    123
Dimensions
    family (Dimension #1), 9–13, 148
    gay male community (GMC)
        (Dimension #3), 39–45
    society (Dimension #2), 15–35, 148
discrimination
    age, 77
    anti-gay bias, 44, 101
    boys and gay, 33
    bullying/mobbing and, 128, 157–158
    hetero-normal and, the, 96
    HIV/AIDS and, 106
    homophobia and, 42, 44
    sexual orientation and, 90
disorders, personality, 117–123
displacement, 140–142
disposable people mentality, 43–44, 150
dissatisfaction/satisfaction. *see*
    satisfaction/dissatisfaction
"don't ask, don't tell" policy, 29, 192
down-low (DL), 43, 139, *164*
DSM (*Diagnostic and Statistical Manual
    of Mental Disorders*), 15, 117–118, 123
dysfunction
    boys and gay, 12–13, 20, 176
    intimacy and, 190
    narcissistic spectrum and, 120–121,
        122, 130, 136
    projection and, 141
    shame and, 25, *35*

E
Eight Stages of Psychosocial
    Development, 20
empathy, 115, 117, *119*, 121, 136, 175–179
environmental dynamics in GMC,
    129–130

Erikson, Erik, 20
esteem, self-, 86, 116, 136
"ethical non-monogamy," 188

F
Facebook, 177
faggot (term), 18, 27, 33, 96
family (Dimension #1), 9–13, 40–41, 148, 192
FDA (Food and Drug Administration, United States), 104
fitness, physical, 69–70
FOMO (fear of missing out), 43–44
Food and Drug Administration, United States (FDA), 104
formation, reaction, 142–143
Freud, Sigmund, 137
"friends with benefits," 188, 189

G
gay male community (GMC) (Dimension #3)
    blocking in, 44
    conformity and, 83–86
    family (Dimension #1) and, 40–41
    HIV/AIDS and, 103–112, *107–108*
    individuality and, 184–185
    intimacy and, 192
    money/wealth (M-Ranking #4) and, 79–81
    M-Ranking System, attitudes toward, 51
    narcissistic spectrum and, 118–131
    society (Dimension #2) and, 40–41
    validation/invalidation in, 39
gay marriage, 89, 191
gay rights movement, 105
gayness, fear of, 42–43
gay-normal, 11, 48
genetics, 123–124, 130–131
GMC (gay male community) (Dimension #3). *see* gay male community (GMC) (Dimension #3)
Grindr, 149

H
hatred of self. *see* self-hatred/self-loathing

have/have-not dynamic, 100, 106, 108, 112
hetero-normal, the
    adolescence and, 19–23
    boys, and gay, 34
    conformity, and gay male, 83–86
    confusion, and role, 21
    defined, term, 11
    denial and, 137–138
    gay male community (GMC) (Dimension #3) and, 40, 53–54
    gay-normal vs., 48
    marriage and, 95
    masculinity (M-Ranking #1) and, 55–56
    parenting and, 1, 9–12
    perfection and, 58
    privilege and, 92–93
    safety and, 17–18
    sexual identity/orientation and, 27, 94–96
    societal norms and, 11
    U-Factor (unblocking factor) and, 173
heteronormative process, 9–10, 17, 27. *see also* hetero-normal, the; heterosexuality
heterosexual male privilege, 89–102
heterosexuality. *see also* hetero-normal, the
    boys and gay, 3–4
    defined, term, 1
    heteronormative process, 9–10, 17, 27
    heterosexism, 57–58
    masculinity (M-Ranking #1) and, 59
    presumptions of, 9–10
    privilege of, 94–95
    school and primary, 17
    sexual identity/orientation and, gay, 59, 155
histrionic personality disorder (HPD), *119*, 120–121, *122*, 143, 144, 152
HIV/AIDS, 103–112, *107–108*
    shame and, 106–107, *109*, 112
homophobia, 39, 42, 55–56, 130–131, 141, 189
homosexuality. *see also* hetero-normal, the; heterosexuality
    choice, as, 155–156
    disorder, as psychological, 15

Index

femininity and, 59
fundamentalism/extremism and, 28
self-denial and, 125, 131
HPD (histrionic personality disorder), *119*, 120–121, *122*, 143–144, 152
humility, 152, 169, *170*, 181–185, *184*

I

identity. *see also* sexual identity/orientation
  boys, and gay, 1, 133
  confusion of, 21, 125, 127, 133–136
  development, 15, 135, 136
  disorders of, 133–136, *135*, *136*
  M-Ranking System and, 134
  penis size and, 64, 66–67
  role confusion and, 20–21
inadequacy
  alcohol and, 150
  boys and gay, 20
  HIV/AIDS and, *109*, 112
  masculinity (M-Ranking #1) and, 71
  M-Ranking System and, *52*, 73
  narcissism and, 123
  penis size and, 71
individuality, 184–185
inequality, 89–90, 92–93
insecurity, 26, 31, 74, 136–137, 141, 144, *147*
insight, 175–179, *178–179*
Instagram, 152, 177
integrity, 181–185, *184*
intimacy, 42–43, 51, 84, 177, 184–185, 187–195, *193*
  shame and, 189, 190
intuition, 175
invalidation/validation. *see* validation/invalidation

L

LGBTQ+ community (lesbian, gay, bisexual, transgender and questioning)
  12-step programs and, 150
  alcohol and, 145
  choice and, 155–156
  closet, and the, 159

defined, term, 1, 2
discrimination and, 90
primary school and, 17
tolerance of, 32
loathing, self-. *see* self-hatred/self-loathing

M

mainstream appeal (M-Ranking #5), 50, 83–86
male perfection. *see* perfection; physical perfection (M-Ranking #3)
male privilege, heterosexual, 89–102
manhood (M-Ranking #2), 49–50, 63–74
marriage
  closet and the, 159, 161, 189
  gay, 89, 191
  hetero-normal and, 95
  intimacy and, 191
  M-Ranking System and, 81
masculinity (M-Ranking #1)
  authenticity and, 58
  benefits of, perceived, 57
  composite assessment of, 60
  delusions and, 144
  disparity and, 100
  introduced, 49
  preference, as, 60–61
  U-Factor (unblocking factor) and, 171
matrix, coming out, *161*
maturity
  ageism and, 77
  alcohol and, 149
  development and arrested, 13
  gay male community (GMC) (Dimension #3), in, 39
  integrity and, 182, 185
  intimacy and, 42, 190, 192
  M-Ranking System and, 75, 171–172
mechanisms, defense, 137–144
mental health. *see also* narcissism; narcissistic spectrum; personality disorders
  identity and, 136
  intimacy and, 190–191
mobbing/bullying. *see* bullying/mobbing

money/wealth (M-Ranking #4), 50, 79–81
monogamy, 195
M-Ranking System
  alcohol and, 150, 152
  authenticity and, 51–52, 58
  explained, 48–54
  inadequacy and, 73
  integrity and, 181, 183–184, 185
  intimacy and, 190, 194–195
  mainstream community (M-Ranking #5), 83–86
  manhood (M-Ranking #2), 63–67
  masculinity (M-Ranking #1), 55–61
  money/wealth (M-Ranking #4), 79–81
  penis size and, 64
  physical perfection (M-Ranking #3), 69–78
  primary, *49*
  transcending the, 199
  U-Factor (unblocking factor) and, 169, 171–172
  value system of, 52
myth of Narcissus, 115

N

narcissism
  alcohol and, 145
  behaviors of, 116–117
  defined, term, 115
  disorders of, 133–136
  gay male community (GMC) (Dimension #3) and, 115–136
  humility and, 185
  integrity and, 185
  shame and, 126–127, 133
  social justice warriors (SJW) and, 177–178
narcissistic personality disorder (NPD), *119*, 120–123, 124
narcissistic spectrum
  alcohol and, 148, 152
  anxiety and, 116, 125–126, 136
  authenticity and, 122, 126
  Cluster B personality disorders and, 118–121
Narcissus, myth of, 115
National Survey on Drug Use and Health:

Lesbian, Gay, or Bisexual (LGB) Adults (2020), 145
normal, gay-, 11, 48
normal, hetero-. see hetero-normal, the
NPD (narcissistic personality disorder), *119*, 120–123, 124

O

"open relationships," 188
orientation, sexual. see sexual identity/ orientation

P

parenting
  boys, and gay, 12–13
  closeted parents, 130–131
  codependency and, 140
  defense mechanisms and, 137–138
  gay-affirmative, 30
  hetero-normal and the, 1, 9–12
  intimacy and, 187–188, 192
  LGBTQ+ community and, 29
  mental health and, 130
  narcissistic spectrum and, 123–124
  role confusion and, 20–21
  shame and, 32–34, 127
  supportive, 26–27
  validation/invalidation and, 26–27, 29–31
passing, privileges of, 99–101
passive aggression, 41, 143
penis size, 63–67
perfection
  in gay male community (GMC), 53–54, 65
  intimacy and, 190, 194–195
  M-Ranking System and, 50, 69–78
  U-Factor (unblocking factor) and, 171
  validation/invalidation and, 124
personality disorders, 117–123, 135, 136, 191. see also *individual disorders*
phobia, HIV-, 109
physical perfection (M-Ranking #3), 50, 69–78
pornography, 65
predispositions for NPD, 123–131
pre-exposure prophylaxis (PrEP), *108*

preference, sexual, masculinity
     (M-Ranking #1) and, 60–61
PrEP (pre-exposure prophylaxis), *108*
privilege
     denial of, 91
     heterosexual male, 89–102
     passing, of, 99–101
     perceptions of, 90–91
     straight male, 89–102
     White privilege, 89–91
projection, 140–142
psychoanalysis, 137

Q
"queen" stereotype, 59
queens, size, 63

R
reaction formation, 142–143
relationship types, 188
repression
     boys and gay, 22–23, 198
     choice and, 155
     defense mechanism, as, 138–139
     intimacy and, 189
     self, of the, 3–4
     sex and, 152
risk factors for NPD, 123–131
role confusion, 20–21

S
safe sex, 109
SAMHSA (Substance Abuse and Mental
     Health Services Administration),
     145
satisfaction/dissatisfaction
     internal, 159, 169–173
     intimacy and, 194
     M-Ranking System and, 51
     social media and, 65–66
     U-Factor (unblocking factor) and, 193
     victim/victimization and, 197
self-acceptance. *see* acceptance
self-centeredness, 146, *147*
self-esteem, 86, 116, 136
self-hatred/self-loathing
     boys and gay, 13

     bullying/mobbing and, 127, 130–131
     closet and the, 141, 159, 162–163
     defense mechanism and, 137
     delusions and, 144
     internalized homophobia and, 55
     shame and, 32
     validation/invalidation and, 27
self-validation. *see* validation/
     invalidation
self-worth/self-respect
     accommodation and, 4, 140, 172
     alcohol and, *147*, 149
     boundaries and, 177
     bullying/mobbing and, 127
     closet and the, 165
     penis size and, 64
     shame and, 25, 31
seroconversion, 104
sex
     gay male community (GMC)
          (Dimension #3), in the, 151–152
     relationships and, 188–189
sexual identity/orientation
     adolescence, in, 19–20
     boys and gay, 198
     choice of, 155–158
     closet and the, 161
     development of, 10, 133, 136
     discrimination and, 101
     hetero-normal and the, 27, 94–96
     heterosexual, 59
     heterosexuality and, 94, 95
     HIV/AIDS and, 118–119
     integrity and, 181
     narcissistic spectrum and, 123, 125
     perpetrators and, 13
     straight passing and, 100
shame
     boundaries and, 176
     boys, and gay, 25–35, *35*
     closet, and the, 165
     HIV/AIDS and, 106–107, *109*, 112
     intimacy and, 189, 190
     narcissism and, 126–127, 133
     substance abuse and, 150
size queens, 63
social climbing, 41, 42, 53, 85, 144, 182

social justice warriors (SJW), 177–178
social media
    bullying/mobbing and, 128
    closet and the, 162–163
    histrionics and, 121
    immediate gratification and, 149
    M-Ranking System and, 58
    narcissism and, 177–178
    pornography and, 65
    projection and, 141
    sexualization and, 151–152
social stigma, 91, 104–106, 108, 110
society (Dimension #2)
    adolescence and, 19–23
    alcohol and, 148
    attitudes toward the GMC, 3, 4–5
    boys and gay, 15–18
    gay male community and, 40–41
    hetero-normal and the, 44
    intimacy and, 192
    shame and, 31–34, *35*
    validation/invalidation and, 25–31
sociopathy, 120, *122*, 138–139, 144
spectrum, narcissistic
    alcohol and, 152
    boys, and gay, 122
    delusions and, 144
    identity confusion and, 133–136
    predispositions for, 123–131
    reaction formation and, 142–143
    risk factors for, 123–131
    traits of, 118–119
stereotypes, 59, 63
stigma
    HIV-positive, 104, 106–107, 108–109, 110
    social, 3, 91, 104, 105, 161, 164
straight-acting privilege. *see* privilege
straight-male privilege. *see* privilege
straight-normal. *see* hetero-normal, the
stress, 126–127, 145, *147*, 149, 165
substance abuse, 43, 129, 145–152, 150, 192
Substance Abuse and Mental Health Services Administration (SAMHSA), 145

T
teachers, 17–18, 32–34
thinking, alcoholic, 145–147
TikTok, 152, 177
tolerance, 15–16
trauma/abuse
    blocking as, 10
    childhood, 4, 13, 15–16, 29, *48*, 126–127
    narcissistic spectrum and, 118–124, 126–127
12-step programs, 149, 150–151
Twitter (X), 177

U
unblocking factor (U-Factor), 4, 169–173, *170*, 199

V
validation/invalidation
    adolescence, in, 29–30
    aggressive invalidation, 28
    boys and gay, 26–31
    continuum, as, 28–29
    defined, term, 25
    gay male community, in, 39
    high validation, 30
    intimacy and, 194
    neutrality, 29–30
    self-validation, 30–31
victims/victimization
    adversity and, 94
    bullying/mobbing and, 126–128
    choice and, 157–158
    reaction formation and, 143
    self-hatred/self-loathing and, 141
    straight-acting privilege and, 102
    straight-male privilege and, *101*
    U-Factor and, *92*, 197

W
White privilege, 89–91
working out, 71–72

X
X (Twitter), 177

About the Author

Joseph Contorer, LMFT, is an author, health educator, and psychotherapist who imparts a pragmatic yet empathic approach to life and therapy. In *You've Been Blocked,* Joseph incorporates his personal, professional, and life experience into a powerful, comprehensive, yet sometimes controversial, critical, edgy discussion.

Joseph's perspective is specifically relevant to growing up in the 1970s and 1980s, entering the gay male community in the 1990s, and working professionally with hundreds of clients during his 30-plus years as a clinician.

Joseph completed his prior education and training in community health education, including a focus on corporate wellness. His experience with health and fitness enhances his approach to addressing mental health as part of a holistic complex. Joseph resides and practices as a licensed marriage and family therapist in California and Oregon and is available for consultation, including national and international telehealth.

Contact Information: Joseph@theblockedbook.com

Made in the USA
Coppell, TX
02 March 2026